# Communications
# in Computer and Information Science     **600**

*Commenced Publication in 2007*
Founding and Former Series Editors:
Alfredo Cuzzocrea, Xiaoyong Du, Orhun Kara, Ting Liu, Dominik Ślęzak,
and Xiaokang Yang

More information about this series at http://www.springer.com/series/7899

Weixia Xu · Liquan Xiao
Jinwen Li · Chengyi Zhang
Zhenzhen Zhu (Eds.)

# Computer Engineering and Technology

21st CCF Conference, NCCET 2017
Xiamen, China, August 16–18, 2017
Revised Selected Papers

 Springer

*Editors*
Weixia Xu
National University of Defense
  Technology
Changsha
China

Liquan Xiao
National University of Defense
  Technology
Changsha
China

Jinwen Li
School of Computer Science
National University of Defense
  Technology
Changsha
China

Chengyi Zhang
National University of Defense
  Technology
Changsha
China

Zhenzhen Zhu
National University of Defense
  Technology
Changsha
China

ISSN 1865-0929          ISSN 1865-0937  (electronic)
Communications in Computer and Information Science
ISBN 978-981-10-7843-9          ISBN 978-981-10-7844-6  (eBook)
https://doi.org/10.1007/978-981-10-7844-6

Library of Congress Control Number: 2017962908

This Springer imprint is published by Springer Nature
The registered company is Springer Nature Singapore Pte Ltd.
The registered company address is: 152 Beach Road, #21-01/04 Gateway East, Singapore 189721, Singapore

# Preface

We are pleased to present the proceedings of the 21st Annual Conference on Computer Engineering and Technology (NCCET 2017). Over its short 20-year history, NCCET has established itself as one of the major national conferences dedicated to the important and emerging challenges in the field of computer engineering and technology. Following the previous successful events, NCCET 2017 provided a forum to bring together researchers and practitioners from academia and industry to discuss cutting-edge research on computer engineering and technology.

We are delighted that the conference continues to attract high-quality submissions from a diverse and national group of researchers. This year, we received 108 paper submissions, among which 13 papers were accepted. Each paper received three or four peer reviews from our Technical Program Committee (TPC) comprising of a total of 55 members from academia and industry.

The pages of this volume represent only the end result of an enormous endeavor involving hundreds of people. Almost all this work is voluntary, with some individuals contributing hundreds of hours of their time to the effort. Together, the 55 members of the TPC, the seven members of the External Review Committee (ERC), and the ten other individual reviewers consulted for their expertise wrote nearly 400 reviews.

Every paper received at least two reviews and many had three or more. With the exception of submissions by the TPC, each paper had at least two reviews from the TPC and at least one review from an outside expert. For the fourth year running, most of the outside reviews were done by the ERC, which was selected in advance, and additional outside reviews beyond the ERC were requested whenever appropriate or necessary. Reviewing was "first read double-blind," meaning that author identities were withheld from reviewers until they submitted a review. Revealing author names after initial reviews were written allowed reviewers to find related and previous material by the same authors, which helped greatly in many cases in understanding the context of the work, and also ensured that the author feedback and discussions at the PC meeting could be frank and direct. We allowed PC members to submit papers to the conference. Submissions co-authored by a TPC member were reviewed exclusively by the ERC and other outside reviewers, and these reviewers decided whether to accept the PC papers or not; no PC member reviewed a TPC paper, and no TPC papers were discussed at the TPC meeting.

After the reviewing was complete, the Program Committee met at the National University of Defense Technology, Changsha, during July 8–9 to select the program. Separately, the ERC decided on the PC papers in e-mail and phone discussions. Finally, 13 of the 108 submissions (12%) were accepted for the conference.

First of all, we would like to thank all researchers who submitted manuscripts. Without these submissions, it would be impossible to provide such an interesting technical program. We thank all PC members for helping to organize the conference program. We thank all TPC members for their tremendous time and efforts during the paper review and selection process. The efforts of these individuals were crucial in constructing our successful technical program. Last but not least, we would like to thank the organizations and sponsors that supported NCCET 2017. Finally, we thank all the participants of the conference and hope that you had a truly memorable NCCET 2017 in Xiamen, China.

November 2017                                              Weixia Xu
                                                       Guo Donghui
                                                     Zhang Minxuan
                                                       Liquan Xiao

# Organization

## General Co-chairs

| | |
|---|---|
| Xu Weixia | National University of Defense Technology, China |
| Guo Donghui | Xiamen University, China |
| Zhang Minxuan | National University of Defense Technology, China |

## Program Chair

| | |
|---|---|
| Xiao Liquan | National University of Defense Technology, China |

## Publicity Co-chairs

| | |
|---|---|
| Zhang Chengyi | National University of Defense Technology, China |
| Li Jinwen | National University of Defense Technology, China |

## Local Arrangements Co-chairs

| | |
|---|---|
| Zhou Jianyang | Xiamen University, China |
| Li Jinwen | National University of Defense Technology, China |

## Registration and Finance Co-chairs

| | |
|---|---|
| Li Yuanshan | National University of Defense Technology, China |
| Zhang Junying | National University of Defense Technology, China |

## Program Committee

| | |
|---|---|
| Han Wei | Xi'an Aviation Institute of Computing Technology, China |
| Jin Lifeng | Jiangnan Institute of Computing Technology, China |
| Xiong Tinggang | 709 Institute of China Shipbuilding Industry, China |
| Zhao Xiaofang | Institute of Computing Technology Chinese Academy of Sciences, China |
| Yang Yintang | Xi Dian University, China |

## Technical Program Committee

| | |
|---|---|
| Jiang Xu | Hong Kong University of Science and Technology, SAR China |
| Liang Huaguo | HeFei University of Technology, China |
| Du Gaoming | HeFei University of Technology, China |
| Chen Yueyue | Hunan Changsha DIGIT Company, China |

| | |
|---|---|
| Dou Qiang | National University of Defense Technology, China |
| Du Huimin | Xi'an University of Posts and Telecommunications, China |
| Fan Dongrui | Institute of Computing Technology Chinese Academy of Sciences, China |
| Fan Xiaoya | Northwestern Polytechnical University, China |
| Fang Xing | Jiangnan Institute of Computing Technology, China |
| Gu Tianlong | Guilin University of Electronic Technology, China |
| Guo Donghui | Xiamen University, China |
| Guo Wei | Tianjin University, China |
| Huang Jin | Xi Dian University, China |
| Han Jun | Fudan University, China |
| Huang Jinming | ICDC, Shanghai, China |
| Ji Liqiang | Cesller Company, China |
| Jin Jie | Hunan Changsha Fusion Company, China |
| Li Ping | University of Electronic Science and Technology of China, China |
| Li Qiong | Inspur Information Technology Co. Ltd., China |
| Li Yuanshan | Inspur Information Technology Co. Ltd., China |
| Li Yun | Yangzhou University, China |
| Liu Yongpan | Tsinghua University, China |
| Lin Kaizhi | Inspur Information Technology Co. Ltd., China |
| Lin Zhenghao | Tongji University, China |
| Meng Jianyi | Zhejiang University, China |
| Jiang Jiang | Shanghai Jiao Tong University |
| Pei Songwen | University of Shanghai for Science and Technology, China |
| Shen Jianliang | Information Engineering University, China |
| Sun Haibo | Inspur Information Technology Co. Ltd., China |
| Sun Yongjie | Hunan Changsha DIGIT Company, China |
| Sun Guangyu | Peking University, China |
| Shi Huibin | Nanjing University of Aeronautics and Astronautics |
| Tian Ze | 631 Institute of AVIC, China |
| Wang Dong | National University of Defense Technology, China |
| Wang Yaonan | Hunan University, China |
| Wang Yiwen | University of Electronic Science and Technology of China, China |
| Xing Zuocheng | Hunan Changsha DIGIT Company, China |
| Xue Chengqi | Southeast University, China |
| Yang Peihe | Jiangnan Institute of Computing Technology, China |
| Yang Xiaojun | Institute of Computing Technology Chinese Academy of Sciences, China |
| Yang Jianxin | ICDC, Shanghai, China |
| Yin Luosheng | Synopsys Company, China |
| Yu Mingyan | Harbin Institute of Technology, China |
| Yu Zongguang | China Electronics Technology Group Corporation NO.58 Research Institute, China |
| Zeng Tian | 709 Institute of China Shipbuilding Industry, China |

| | |
|---|---|
| Zeng Xifang | Hunan Great Wall Information Technology Co. Ltd., China |
| Zeng Yu | Sugon Company, China |
| Zeng Yun | Hunan University, China |
| Zhang Jianyun | PLA Electronic Engineering Institute, China |
| Zhang Lixin | Institute of Computing Technology Chinese Academy of Sciences, China |
| Zhang Shengbing | Northwestern Polytechnical University, China |
| Zhang Xu | Jiangnan Institute of Computing Technology, China |
| Zhang Yiwei | 709 Institute of China Shipbuilding Industry, China |
| Zhao Yuelong | South China University of Technology, China |
| Zhou Ya | Guilin University of Electronic Technology, China |

# Contents

# A Low TC Voltage Reference Generator Suitable for Low Temperature Applications

Jianguo Hu[1(✉)], Jiangxu Wu[2], and Ge Lin[3]

[1] School of Data and Computer Science, Sun Yat-Sen University,
Guangzhou, China
hujguo@mail.sysu.edu.cn
[2] School of Electronics and Information Technology,
Sun Yat-Sen University, Guangzhou, China
wujx27@mail2.sysu.edu.cn
[3] Sun Yat-Sen University, Guangzhou, China

**Abstract.** A low temperature coefficient (TC) CMOS voltage reference generator suitable for low temperature is proposed. It exploits temperature mutual compensation relationship between threshold voltage and thermal voltage, and provides a mean reference voltage of 692 mV. A proportional to absolute temperature (PTAT) current containing the thermal voltage which has a positive TC is generated, and then it is injected into a diode-connected NMOS transistor that supply the threshold voltage which has a negative TC. The mixing of the two voltages produces a reference voltage with zero TC. The proposed circuit is implemented with SMIC CMOS 0.18 um process technology. The simulation results show that the power consumption is 2.1 uW and the TC is 9.3 ppm/°C. The temperature range is from −75°C to 65°C, which indicates that the proposed circuit can be applied in low temperature environment.

**Keywords:** Voltage reference · Low TC · CMOS · Subthreshold voltage

## 1 Introduction

The IoT (Internet of Things) carries on the information exchange and the communication through internet, in order to realize the object recognition, localization, tracking, monitoring and management. RFID (Radio Frequency Identification) is the key technologies of the IoT that enable automatic identification and management of specific object in a variety of situations [1]. However, many RFID tags can not work well in many high latitudes because of low temperature. This leads to RFID applications being hindered in these regions. Therefore, it is necessary to develop a RFID tag suitable for low temperature applications.

Many voltage reference circuits were proposed. The most commonly used method is the bandgap voltage reference, where a CTAT (complementary to absolute temperature) source is balanced by a PTAT (proportional to absolute temperature) source, resulting in the silicon bandgap voltage as the reference voltage. Some advanced bandgap voltage references based on parasitic bipolar transistor with lower power consumption than the traditional bandgap reference is invented [2]. Meanwhile, voltage reference circuits based on the fact that the threshold voltage of transistor with different gate oxide thickness in the same CMOS technology exhibit different temperature characteristic is proposed [3], but it requires additional fabrication steps. Recently, the dependence of $V_{th}$ with respect to the channel length is exploited in order to obtain different $V_{th}$ is proposed [4], however, its temperature range is very small and is not suitable for low temperature environment. The subthreshold characteristics of transistors have been widely exploited in the field of reference voltage. In this way, voltage difference between the gate-source of two transistors operating in the subthreshold region were used to generate a PTAT voltage [5]. A novel voltage reference is introduced in [6, 7], it consists of standard transistors operating in subthreshold regime. It generates a threshold voltage with negative TC and a multiple of the thermal voltage with positive TC, and then adds them to produce a voltage reference with zero TC. But its temperature coefficients are not ideal.

In this work, we propose a novel voltage reference circuit. It generates a PTAT current containing the thermal voltage with a positive TC and then injected into a diode-connected NMOS transistor which supplies the threshold voltage with a negative TC to achieve an output voltage reference near zero TC. Simulation results show that this work has low TC and wide temperature range that from $-75\,°C$ to $65\,°C$. Thus it can be used in extremely cold conditions.

## 2 Circuit Design

The architecture of the proposed voltage reference generator is shown in Fig. 1. It consists of a current generator and an active load. The current generator formed by transistors number from M1 to M10 generates a PTAT current $I_0$. Such current is

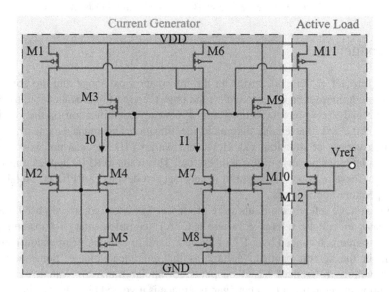

**Fig. 1.** The proposed circuit

injected into the active load that formed by M11 and M12 to generate the reference voltage $V_{ref}$. The current $I_0$ and the gate-source voltage of M12 that are dependence of temperature are compensate each other, then the $V_{ref}$ is independence of temperature.

All the transistors except for M4, M5, M7 and M8 are operated in the saturation. The M4 and M7 are operated in the subthreshold region, and the M5 and M8 are operated in deep triode region. The core of the current generator circuit is represented by transistors M2, M4, M5, M7, M8 and M10, which determine the value of the current $I_0$. Meanwhile the current mirror consisted by M3 and M9 supply equal current $I_0$ in M4, M5 and M10, and the current mirror consisted by M1 and M6 supply equal current $I_1$ in M2, M7 and M8. It is a very important point in the design that the current $I_0$ and $I_1$ are equal by adjusting the parameters of the transistor. The current-voltage characteristic of a transistor that operates in the subthreshold region and in the subthreshold region can be approximated by (1) and (2), respectively.

$$I_D = \frac{\mu C_{ox}}{2} K(V_{GS} - V_{TH})^2 (1 + \lambda V_{DS}) \tag{1}$$

$$I_D = KI \exp\left(\frac{V_{GS} - V_{TH}}{mV_T}\right) \times \left[1 - \exp\left(-\frac{V_{DS}}{V_T}\right)\right] \tag{2}$$

where $K$ is the aspect ratio ($= W/L$) of the transistor ($W$ and $L$ are the channel width and length), $V_{GS}$ and $V_{DS}$ are the gate-source voltage and the drain-source voltage, respectively. $I = \mu C_{ox}(m - 1)V_T^2$, $\mu$ is the electron mobility in the channel, $C_{ox}$ is the gate-oxide capacitance, $V_T = (K_B T/q)$ is the thermal voltage ($K_B$ is the Boltzmann constant, $T$ is the absolute temperature, and $q$ is the elementary charge), $V_{TH}$ is the threshold voltage, $\lambda$ is the channel length modulation coefficient, and $m$ is the subthreshold slope factor. The gate-source voltages of M2 (M10) that operates in saturation with drain current $I_1$ ($I_0$) can be extracted from (1) and of M4 (M7) that operates in subthreshold with drain current $I_0$ ($I_1$) can be extracted from (2). Then we have,

$$\begin{cases} V_{GS4} - V_{th4} = mV_T \ln\dfrac{I_0}{K_4 I} \\[2mm] V_{GS2} - V_{th2} = \sqrt{\dfrac{2I_1}{\mu_n C_{ox} K_2}} \end{cases} \tag{3}$$

$$\begin{cases} V_{GS10} - V_{th10} = mV_T \ln\dfrac{I_0}{K_{10} I} \\[2mm] V_{GS7} - V_{th7} = \sqrt{\dfrac{2I_1}{\mu_n C_{ox} K_7}} \end{cases} \tag{4}$$

Where we neglect the channel length modulation of M2 and M10 since they are long channel devices. Meanwhile, we also can set the second square brackets in Eq. (2) to unity when $V_{DS} \geq 0.1V$ is met [7]. Obviously, because the source of M2 and M10 are grounded, and the source of M4 and M7 are connected with each other, the body effect plays no role and we have $V_{th4} = V_{th7}$ and $V_{th10} = V_{th2}$. By subtracting the upper from the lower in Eqs. (3) and (4), we can get the following two equations.

$$V_{GS2} - V_{GS4} = V_{th2} - V_{th4} + \sqrt{\frac{2I_1}{\mu_n C_{ox} K_2}} - mV_T \ln\frac{I_0}{K_4 I} \tag{5}$$

$$V_{GS10} - V_{GS7} = V_{th10} - V_{th7} + \sqrt{\frac{2I_0}{\mu_n C_{ox} K_{10}}} - mV_T \ln\frac{I_1}{K_7 I} \tag{6}$$

Because the drain of the transistor M5 and M8 are connected, the drain potential of them is equal. The left side of the Eqs. (5) and (6) equals the drain voltage of the transistor M5 and M8, respectively. Therefore, the right side of Eqs. (5) and (6) is equal. By subtracting (5) from (6), we can extract the expression of the current $I_0$.

$$I_0 = \frac{\mu_n C_{ox} m^2 V_T^2 \ln^2\left(\frac{K_7}{K_4}\right)}{2\left(\frac{1}{K_2} + \frac{1}{K_{10}}\right) - 4\sqrt{\frac{1}{K_2 K_{10}}}} \tag{7}$$

What we needs to be explained is that the two currents $I_0$ and $I_1$ are equal not realized by an electric current mirror, but by adjusting the parameters of the circuit. From Eq. (7) we can found some conditions need to be satisfied that it is $K_2 \neq K_{10}$ and $K_7 \neq K_4$. When the gate potential of M5 and M8 is different, the same drain current of the M2 and M10 and $K_2 \neq K_{10}$ can be satisfied at the same time. Obviously, the gate source voltages of M4 and M7 are also different. However, the drain currents of M4 and M7 are the same which make the condition $K_7 \neq K_4$ is established.

The current $I_0$ is then mirrored into the diode connected transistor M12 through M11 to get a temperature compensated reference voltage. The relationship between the drain current of M12 and the current $I_0$ can be obtained by M3 and M11. The transistor M12 operates in the saturation region and the reference voltage can be expressed as (8).

$$V_{ref} = V_{th12} + \left|mV_T \ln\left(\frac{K_7}{K_4}\right)\right| \sqrt{\frac{K_{11}}{K_{12} K_3 \left[\left(\frac{1}{K_2} - \frac{1}{K_{10}}\right) - 2\sqrt{\frac{1}{K_2 K_{10}}}\right]}} \tag{8}$$

The channel length modulation effect is mainly related to the drain source voltage and can be avoided by the diode-connected form. The best way to drastically reduce the channel length effect is to increase the parameter L. Thus, the channel length of all the transistors in the current mirrors and of M5, M8 must be quite large. Meanwhile, the drain-source voltage of M4, M7 which operate in the subthreshold region must be much large than the thermal voltage to eliminate the dependence of current on $V_{DS}$ in (2).

## 3  Supply Voltage Dynamic Range

The minimum supply voltage is determined by the current generator circuit. In particular, we have to meet the condition that $V_{DSS} < V_{GS5} - V_{th5}$ to ensure the M5 operates in the deep triode region, and the drain-source voltage of M4 larger than

100 mV, and that M3 operates in saturated with $|V_{GS3}| > V_{th5}$. Consequently, the following expression has to be satisfied,

$$V_{DD} > |V_{GS3}| + V_{DS4} + V_{DS5} \qquad (9)$$

Simulation results show that the supply voltage must be larger than 1 V in the SMIC 0.18 um CMOS process. Such voltage is also sufficient to ensure the M2 operates in the saturation region. The maximum supply voltage is determined by the maximum drain-source voltage allowed for M11, thus we have,

$$V_{DD} < |V_{DS11MAX}| + V_{ref} \qquad (10)$$

Since the maximum drain-source voltage of a transistor is 1.8 V in the SMIC 0.18 um CMOS process. As a result, the maximum supply voltage of the circuit is about 2.5 V.

## 4  Temperature Compensation

As an approximation, we can consider that the temperature dependence of the threshold voltage can be given by (11).

$$V_{TH}(T) = V_{TH}(T_0) + \alpha(T - T_0) \qquad (11)$$

where $T_0$ is the reference temperature which is $300°K$ and $\alpha$ is a negative value [8]. Substituting Eq. (11) and $V_T = K_B T / q$ in Eq. (8), the reference voltage $V_{ref}$ can be rewritten as:

$$V_{ref} = V_{th12}(T_0) + \alpha(T - T_0) + \left| m \frac{K_B T}{q} \ln\left(\frac{K_7}{K_4}\right) \right| \sqrt{\frac{K_{11}}{K_{12}K_3\left[\left(\frac{1}{K_2} + \frac{1}{K_{10}}\right) - 2\sqrt{\frac{1}{K_2 K_{10}}}\right]}} \qquad (12)$$

By differentiating (12) with respect to the temperature on can obtains,

$$\frac{\partial V_{ref}}{\partial T} = \alpha + m \frac{K_B}{q} \left| \ln\left(\frac{K_7}{K_4}\right) \right| \sqrt{\frac{K_{11}}{K_{12}K_3\left[\left(\frac{1}{K_2} + \frac{1}{K_{10}}\right) - 2\sqrt{\frac{1}{K_2 K_{10}}}\right]}} \qquad (13)$$

As we can see from (13), the TC is independent of the carrier mobility which dependence of temperature. Thus, the temperature dependence of the mobility is suppressed due to the topological structure of the circuit. This leads to a smaller TC compared to the mobility is introduced at the reference voltage. By setting (13) to zero, we obtain the condition (14).

$$-\alpha = m\frac{K_B}{q}\left|\ln\left(\frac{K_7}{K_4}\right)\right|\sqrt{\frac{K_{11}}{K_{12}K_3\left[\left(\frac{1}{K_2}+\frac{1}{K_{10}}\right)-2\sqrt{\frac{1}{K_2K_{10}}}\right]}} \tag{14}$$

If (14) is satisfied, the Eq. (13) will be equal to zero for any temperature. As shown in Fig. 2, across the temperature from −75 °C to 65 °C, the total variation of the reference voltage is only about 0.9 mV and the TC is 9.3 ppm/°C which shows a good insensitivity to the temperature.

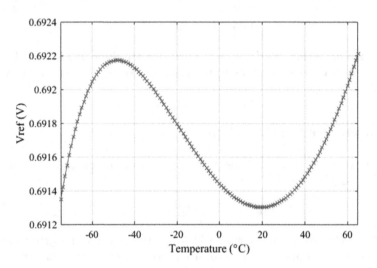

**Fig. 2.** The reference voltage $V_{ref}$ versus temperature

## 5   Channel Length Modulation Effect

The Eq. (7) will be recalculated if we take the channel length modulation effect into account. The I-V characteristics of a MOS in the saturation region and in the sub-threshold region can be written as in (1) for $\lambda \neq 0$ and as in (2) for $\exp(-V_{DS}/V_T) \neq 0$. we only need to consider the channel length modulation effect on M4 and M7, because of M2 and M10 is diode-connected. Under such conditions, using the same procedure to recalculate the Eq. (7), the current $I_0$ is expressed by (15).

$$I_0 = \frac{\mu_n C_{ox}m^2 V_T^2}{2\left(\frac{1}{\sqrt{K_2}}-\frac{1}{\sqrt{K_{10}}}\right)^2}\ln^2\left[\frac{K_7}{K_4}\frac{1-\exp(-\frac{V_{DS7}}{V_T})}{1-\exp(-\frac{V_{DS4}}{V_T})}\right] \tag{15}$$

By using first-order Taylor series expansion to rewrite (15),

$$I_0 = I_{0NOM}\left[1+\ln\left(\frac{K_4}{K_7}\frac{V_{DS7}}{V_{DS4}}\right)\right]^2 \tag{16}$$

Where $I_{0NOM}$ is the current $I_0$ when the channel length modulation effect is neglected $(\exp(-V_{DS}/V_T) = 0)$. By using (8) and (16), the reference voltage can be rewritten as (17).

$$V_{ref} = V_{ref0} + m\frac{K_B T}{q}\left|\ln\left(\frac{K_7}{K_4}\right)\right|\left|\sqrt{\frac{K_{11}K_2K_{10}}{K_{12}K_3}}\frac{1}{\sqrt{K_{10}} - \sqrt{K_2}}\right|\left(\left|1 + \ln\left(\frac{K_4}{K_7}\frac{V_{DS7}}{V_{DS4}}\right)\right| - 1\right) \quad (17)$$

Where $V_{ref0}$ is the reference voltage calculated by (8). The drain-source voltage of M4 and M7 can be expressed by (18) and (19).

$$V_{DS4} = V_{DD} - \left|\frac{2I_0}{\mu_p C_{ox}K_4} + |V_{tp4}|\right| - V_{DS5} \quad (18)$$

$$V_{DS7} = V_{DD} - \left|\frac{2I_0}{\mu_p C_{ox}K_7} + |V_{tp7}|\right| - V_{DS8} \quad (19)$$

Where $V_{tp}$ is the threshold voltage of a PMOS transistor. Because the drain terminal of M5 and M8 are connect with each other, we have $V_{DS5} = V_{DS8}$. By assuming that $K_4 = K_7$, then $V_{DS4} = V_{DS7}$. We can rewrite (17) as $V_{ref} = V_{ref0}$. Thus the channel length modulation effect can be compensated by setting $K_4 = K_7$ in the proposed voltage reference. Thanks to the topology used and to proper dimensioning, the channel length modulation is compensated, leading to a very good temperature coefficient.

## 6  Experimental Results

To verify the performance of the proposed design, we use the SPICE simulator to simulate the circuit with SMIC 0.18 um CMOS process. Measurements show that the proposed voltage reference generates a mean reference voltage of about 692 mV with a variation of 50 mV at all corner, when the temperature varies from −75 °C to 65 °C, as shown in Fig. 3. The PSRR (power supply rejection ratio), without any filtering capacitor, is −41.5 dB at 1 kHz and −31.3 dB at 10 MHz when VDD = 1 V, and decreases to −49.7 dB at 1 kHz and to −36.1 dB at 10 MHz when VDD = 1.8 V, as shown in Fig. 4. Figure 5 shows the output reference voltage versus VDD at all corner. With VDD ranging from 1 to 2.5 V, the measured line sensitivity is 1.9%/V at TT corner. In order to evaluate the sensitivity of the reference voltage to process variations, Monte Carlo analysis assuming WID mismatch variations in all MOSFETs were considered. Figure 6 shows the distribution of average output voltage $V_{ref}$ at 1 V power supply. We assumed a Gaussian distribution $(\delta_{vth})$ for the WID variation. The average voltage $V_{ref}$ was about 691.7995 mV in this simulation. The coefficient of variation $(\delta/\mu)$ in 30 runs was 0.48%. Figure 7 shows Monte Carlo simulation with 30 different samples of the reference voltage. Table 1 summarize the main performance of the proposed circuit and compares with previous works.

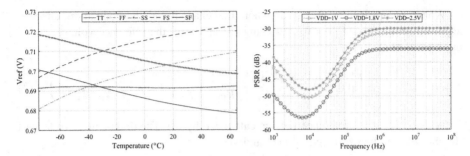

**Fig. 3.** Measured $V_{ref}$ at all corners          **Fig. 4.** The PSRR at different supply power

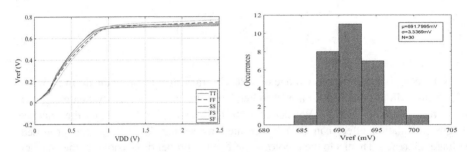

**Fig. 5.** The reference voltage $V_{ref}$ versus **Fig. 6.** Distribution of $V_{ref}$ for 30-point supply
voltage at all corner                              Monte Carlo simulations

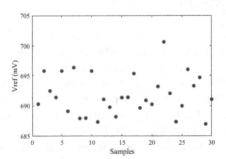

**Fig. 7.** Monte Carlo simulation with 30 samples

**Table 1.** Performance comparison

| | [4] | [5] | [6] | [7] | This work |
|---|---|---|---|---|---|
| Supply voltage (V) | 0.3–1.2 | 0.45–1.8 | 1–3 | 0.3 | 1–2.5 |
| Technology (nm) | 130 | 180 | 180 | 65 | 180 |
| Power | 7 pW | 18.7 nW | 0.23 uW | 70 nW | 2.1 uW |
| Vref (mV) | 85 | 118.41 | 610 | 168 | 692 |
| PSRR | −18 dB @100 Hz | −50.3 dB @100 Hz | −15.4 dB @10 MHz | | −49.7 dB@1 kHz −36.1 dB@10 MHz |
| Temperature range (°C) | 0–120 | −40–85 | −40–120 | −20–100 | −75–65 |
| TC (ppm/°C) | 17.4 | 59.4 | 66.9 | 142 | 9.3 |

## 7 Conclusion

A novel approach for low TC and wide temperature range voltage reference generator is presented. The proposed circuit has been implemented in SMIC 0.18 um CMOS process with the reference voltage of 692 mV. Due to the topology used and to proper dimensioning, channel length modulation and body effect are compensated, leading to a very good temperature coefficient of 9.3 ppm/°C. Monte Carlo simulation show a $\delta/\mu = 0.48\%$ spread for reference voltage, when considering both average process and mismatch variations. The circuit can work well under the temperature varies from −75 °C to 65 °C. This shows that the circuit can work in extremely cold high latitudes.

**Acknowledgments.** The research is supported by the National Natural Science Foundation of China (No. 61402546), the research is also supported by the Science and Technology Program of Guangzhou, China (No. 201604010110) and the Science and Technology Program of Guangzhou, China (No. 201604016126).

## References

1. Park, S.: A development of UHF RFID device for mobile IoT service. In: UEMCON 2016, pp. 1–7. IEEE (2016)
2. Sanborn, K., Ma, D., Ivanov, V.: A Sub-1-V low noise bandgap voltage reference. IEEE J. Solid-State Circuits **42**, 2466–2481 (2007)
3. Yang, Z., Jiang, M.: Nanopower CMOS voltage reference circuit with 16 ppm/°C from 0°C to 150°C without resistors. In: ICCE-TW, pp. 424–425. IEEE (2015)
4. de Oliveira, A.C., Caicedo, J.G.: 0.3 V supply, 17 ppm/°C 3-transistor picowatt voltage reference. In: LASCAS, pp. 263–266. IEEE (2016)
5. Zhu, Z., Hu, J., Wang, Y.: A 0.45 V, nan0-watt 0.033% line sensitivity MOSFET-only subthreshold voltage reference with no amplifiers. IEEE Trans. Circuits Syst. I Regul. Pap. **63**, 1370–1380 (2016)
6. Li, J., Li, J. and Yang, L.: A nanopower, high PSRR full CMOS voltage reference circuit consisting of subthreshold MOSFETs. In: ASICON, pp. 1–4. IEEE (2015)

7. Lu, T.C., Ker, M.D., Zan, H.W.: A 70nW, 0.3 V temperature compensation voltage reference consisting of subthreshold MOSFETs in 65 nm CMOS technology. In: VLSI-DAT, pp. 1–4. IEEE (2016)
8. Ueno, K.: A 300 nW, 15 ppm/°C, 20 ppm/V CMOS voltage reference circuit consisting of subthreshold MOSFETs. IEEE J. Solid-State Circuits **44**, 2047–2054 (2009)
9. Filanovsky, I.M., Allam, A.: Mutual compensation of mobility and threshold voltage temperature effects with application in CMOS circuits. IEEE Trans. Circuits Syst. I Fundam. Theory and Appl. **48**, 876–884 (2001)

# A Java Card Virtual Machine Design Based on Off-card/On-card Co-design Pre-processing

Jiaxin Hong[✉], Jianguo Hu, and Ge Lin

School of Data and Computer Science, Sun Yat-Sen University,
Guangzhou, China
hongjx3@mail2.sysu.edu.cn, hujguo@mail.sysu.edu.cn

**Abstract.** The design of Java Card Virtual Machine (JCVM) is the critical part in Java Card development. One of the evaluation standards on Java card is the fast response rate. Embedded a high performance JCVM on the memory constrained devices such as smart card is a great challenge. This paper presents an implementation of JCVM and an off-card/on-card co-design pre-processing approach to speed up the interpreter in JCVM. In the off-card domain, we propose moving part of instruction interpreting off card, performing a static analysis on applet files before downloaded. In the on-card domain, a dynamic analysis for external items reference is adopted with a small amount of addition code. The experiment result shows that our proposed scheme has an improvement of 36.3% on execution rate, therefore it is effective to speed up JCVM and it is available for Java card to raise its responsive efficiency.

**Keywords:** Java Card Virtual Machine (JCVM) · Interpreter
Off-card/on-card co-design · Pre-processing

## 1 Introduction

Java card is nowadays a development trend of smart cards. It is widely used in the field of finance, identification, transportation and mobile communication. Compared with the native card, Java card can support for multiple applications and provide higher security. Java card specification is a reduced version of Java because of its memory constrained [1–3]. One of the important component of Java card is Java card virtual machine (JCVM), which bridges between the underlying hardware and card applications [4]. The causes for the slow development of Java card include a lack of a large memory chip and a high efficiency JCVM. Therefore, realizing a JCVM with higher execution rate is significant.

Many researches on high performance JCVM have applied JVM optimization algorithms to JCVM. The interpreter in traditional JCVM uses switch-case approach to invoke instructions' handler functions. This method is simple and clean but greatly slows down the execution speed of the interpreter. The most common optimization method for virtual machine is direct threaded interpreter proposed by Ertl in [5]. It utilizes a threaded array to record a series of instructions' handler address, which are converted from executed bytecode and remain operand unchanged. The interpreter now can just execute threaded array without switching and the execution speed can be

© Springer Nature Singapore Pte Ltd. 2018
W. Xu et al. (Eds.): NCCET 2017, CCIS 600, pp. 11–21, 2018.
https://doi.org/10.1007/978-981-10-7844-6_2

improved greatly. In [6] Gregg et al. uses this method into Java system and it presents a amazing result. However, a handler address needs 32-bit memory in ARM micropro-cessor which is four times larger than an instruction. It is not suitable for smart card to implement.

Jin et al. in [7] propose reducing times of writing EEPROM to raise execution rate. The authors provide two methods to realize it. One is to implement transaction pro-cessing in RAM and the other is to set a Java card object buffer with high locality.

In [8] Zilli et al. design a hardware and software co-design scheme to improve execute rate of JCVM. They integrate part of the interpreter to the microprocessor. Their optimal JCVM architecture is to fetch and decode on hardware and execute with software.

The author Liu et al. in [9] work on instruction folding on Java card. They use shift-reduce method to recognize and fold several instructions into one new instruction defined by authors. The result they presents that this method can reach a gain of 1.24 on financial applet.

The off-card approach is not only instruction folding algorithm, CAO and Ying in [10] research on instruction pre-scheduling algorithm. They analyzed executed instruction flow from applets and then proposed a code arrangement method to realize the pre-scheduling of interpreter. This method has took the program locality into consideration and has increased efficiency of interpreter by improving cache hit rate.

The solutions proposed above can have a good improvement on JCVM. However, using a buffer in RAM memory needs a large amount of memory overhead. Imple-menting on hardware has high hardware requirement such that it will limit the appli-cation and extension. The result of the off-card optimization methods such as instruction folding and instruction pre-scheduling are vary from applet to applet. Thus their running JCVM should be adjusted according to the processing result of each applet such that these approaches are not suitable for multiple applets. Thus, a method that can balance memory cost and execution time for multiple applets in Java card is rarely found.

In the solution that we propose in this paper we combine the off-card and the on-card pre-processing method based on applet file to realize a high efficiency JCVM. In terms of the off-card aspect, we perform a static analysis on constant pool array and the size of the output file will not be changed. As for the on-card aspect we perform a dynamic analysis in order to reference to another applet in card. After optimization, the instructions executing can directly get the offset or address by constant pool array rather than a long time linking process, which can greatly decrease the running time of JCVM.

This paper is organized as follows. Section 2 introduces the framework of the proposed JCVM design and the implementation of each module. Section 3 gives the detail description of the optimization scheme based on applet file. Section 4 shows the experiment result of comparison before and after optimization. Section 5 makes a conclusion for this work.

## 2   JCVM Implementation

The virtual machine of Java card is divided into the off-card part and the on-card part. In this paper, we focus on the on-card JCVM, which is responsible for interpreting and executing. The optimization of JCVM is based on the implementation of JCVM. In this section, we first introduce the system architecture of JCVM and the design of each modules.

### 2.1   System Architecture

The core of JCVM is the interpreter whose duty is to fetch, decode and execute instructions. The interpreter has four modules, including stack management module, heap management module, register management module and execution module. The execution module works as a core and the rest are auxiliary modules. RAM is used to store Java stack, register and other runtime data structure. EEPROM is used to store object of different card applets and some other persistent objects. Figure 1 shows the complete framework of the designed interpreter in JCVM.

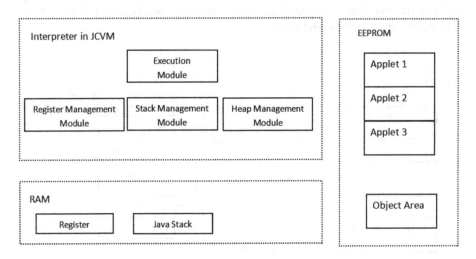

**Fig. 1.** Overview of the designed interpreter in JCVM

### 2.2   Execution Module

Traditional interpreter in JCVM uses switch-case to decode and execute instruction after the fetch step. An instruction handler should be found from case zero to the target case. When next instruction was fetched, the program jumped back to the beginning of the loop and find the next target case. This mechanism is time consuming since it has accessed memory twice and jumped once. First memory access is to fetch instruction and the second is to find handler in switch-case.

Unfortunately, direct threaded interpreter is not suitable in smart card, thus in this paper, we use a handler table as a tool for interpreter. The handler table and the instructions are one-to-one relationship. Each element in table stores the instruction handling function address. The instructions provided by Java card specification are numbered from 0 to 184 as operation code such that they can be easily corresponded to the array index. When executing bytecode, we use instruction's operation code as index to get its handler address. This method can obviously reduce the instruction matching time.

## 2.3   Runtime Data Area

During the process of executing bytecode, the interpreter stores internal data in stack. JCVM runs only one thread thus it only needs one stack in RAM. Java stack is consisted of several frames. Each frame is corresponding to a method invoked. The stack management module is responsible for frame creating, frame pushing and popping. The structure of frame contains three parts: operand stack, local variable area and runtime environment. When VM executes a method invoked by an instruction, it will create a frame and push it into the Java stack. The frame of this method will be pop until this method returns. Figure 2 shows the runtime data area of JCVM and the relationship between frame and register.

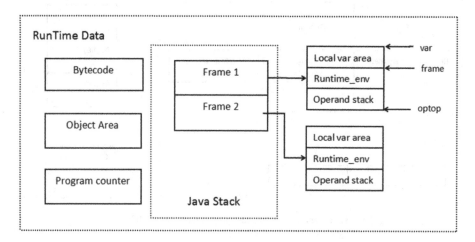

**Fig. 2.**  Runtime data of JCVM

As shown in Fig. 2, there are all four registers needed in JCVM. Three of them record address of data area in frame. Register optop stores the address at the top of the operand stack in the current frame; Register var stores the starting address of local variable area in the current frame; Register frame stores the starting address of runtime environment in the current frame. The rest one register is program counter (pc). It records the address of the executing instruction. Register management module is in charge of these four registers, including initializing, getting and setting registers' value.

Each method invoked by interpreter uses a frame to store internal data. Local variable area is used for passing parameters. Operand stack is used to store calculating data. For example, before the arithmetic computations, the interpreter will first execute two instructions that load two variables to operand stack. Then it comes to an arithmetic instruction, interpreter will pop two values from stack and then push back the computing result. Runtime environment in a frame is used to store information of the caller method.

The duties of stack management module are initializing frame, creating frame, and pushing or popping frame. When a method is called, method arguments will be popped from caller's operand stack and passed to the callees storing in the local variable area of callee. In Java stack, callee's frame adjoins caller's frame and caller's operand stack is next to callee's local variable area. Therefore, in this paper we use Frame Memory Sharing approach to remove the argument passing process. The method makes part of caller's operand stack overlap with part of callee's local variable area such that they share part of data and need not to pass argument. Figure 3 shows the detail of Frame Memory Sharing design.

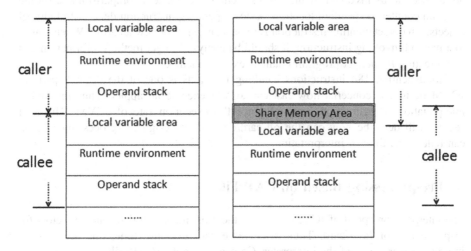

**Fig. 3.** The design of Frame Memory Sharing

Using this approach, the caller only need to push the passing argument into operand stack and the frame created for the callee can start at the sharing area. It is realized by moving registers. When a new frame create, the registers can be set by following formulas.

$$cur\_var = pre\_optop - cur\_methodParaSize; \qquad (1)$$

$$cur\_frame = pre\_optop + max\_locals; \qquad (2)$$

$$cur\_optop = cur\_frame + FRAME\_SIZE; \qquad (3)$$

The Frame Memory Sharing approach can save not only space of Java stack but also time of passing arguments. When the callee returns, the frame of callee is deleted including sharing area, and then the return value of callee will push into caller's operand stack.

### 2.4  Implementation of Instruction Handlers

Each method of card applet is stored in method component. It is consist of instructions specified in JCVM specification. An instruction has a single byte operating code, numbers from 0 to 184. After operating code is several bytes of operand. There are seven kinds of instructions: load, store, branch, field operating, object creating and method invoking. A load instruction is to push a value into operand stack. The value may access from local variable area or instruction operand. A store instruction is to popping value from operand stack and store into local variable area. An arithmetic instruction will pop the value to be calculated from operand stack and pushing back the computing result. The types of value used in calculating are short and int. Reference is not allowed to be involved. A branch instruction is to make a comparison and set the program counter to specified location. A field operating instruction deals with fields of objects. An object creating instruction is to new an object or new an array. When comes to a method invoking instruction, it should be analyzed to get method information and then creating frame, set program counter, execute method.

Implementing 184 instructions handling functions is one of the difficult parts in JCVM design. It concerns how fast can JCVM execute an applet. Thus improving interpretation of instructions can influence the execution rate of JCVM. The next section will describe how can the off-card/on-card co-design pre-processing method can reduce the time of interpretation.

## 3  Pre-processing Based on CAP File

The interpretaion speed of JCVM is one of the most important determinate factors for response rate of Java card. Thus to decrease card response time, one access is to improve performance of the interpreter. Converted Applet (CAP) file is an executable binary file represented for card applet. Our optimization approach for JCVM is a pre-processing method is based on CAP file. In this section we present a detail implementation of the off-card/on-card pre-processing. Before that, we introduce some basic knowledge of linking process scheme in order to have a better understanding of the whole optimization approach.

### 3.1  Static Analysis and Dynamic Analysis

In Java card, there is a token-based linking scheme such that card applet can be linked to Java card API embedded on the card. When applet converted, every external visible item will be assigned a public token which can be referenced from another card applet. One applet is related to one package. In a package there are three types items can be assigned public tokens, including classes, methods and fields. When JCVM executes bytecode in method component, some instructions require interpreter to change these tokens into corresponding address or offset, and this process is called instruction analysis. There are two kinds of instruction analysis: static analysis (SA) and dynamic analysis (DA). It is according to whether the analysis is involved external package or just local package.

SA only needs local component. The instruction operand in method component refer to constant pool component, and then refer to class component or static field component according to the specified instruction. DA needs information from other packages, such as linking to API. It can be seen that DA rely on resources in Java card so it must be done on the card. Instruction analysis is the key module in JCVM execution therefore improving efficiency of interpreter will have a considerable result for the whole Java card performance.

### 3.2    Implementation of Pre-processing

In CAP file, constant pool array in constant pool component contains an element for each class, method, field referenced by items in method component of this CAP file [2]. These reference information link to entry in class component, method component, static field component and import component. When executing some instructions such as method invoking instruction which need linking processing, JCVM can get reference information by accessing constant pool array.

The CAP file pre-processing proposed in this paper is based on analyzing of constant pool array, including off-card SA and on-card DA.

**Off-card SA Implementation.** Off-card SA is performed by a program. The input is CAP file and output is also a CAP file with the same size. Usually, those instructions that need to be analyzed have one or two bytes operand as an index to constant pool array and get an entry. This entry has 4-byte information. The first byte is a tag, showing that if this entry is a class, a method or a field. If it is a class, then the following are 2-byte class index and 1-byte padding. If it is a method, then the following are 2-byte class index and 1-byte method token. Using these reference information JCVM can locate the position of method, class or field and then replace into constant pool array. Take method invoke instruction as example.

1. When executing an instruction, taking its operand as an index to constant pool array and get a 4-byte information cp;
2. Assume that $cp_0$ shows the entry is a method, then the next 2-byte token is a class token.
3. Located in class component according to the class token and get the method offset with method token in $cp_3$;
4. Replace the entry in constant pool array with this method;

Figure 4 shows the off-card pre-processing operation.

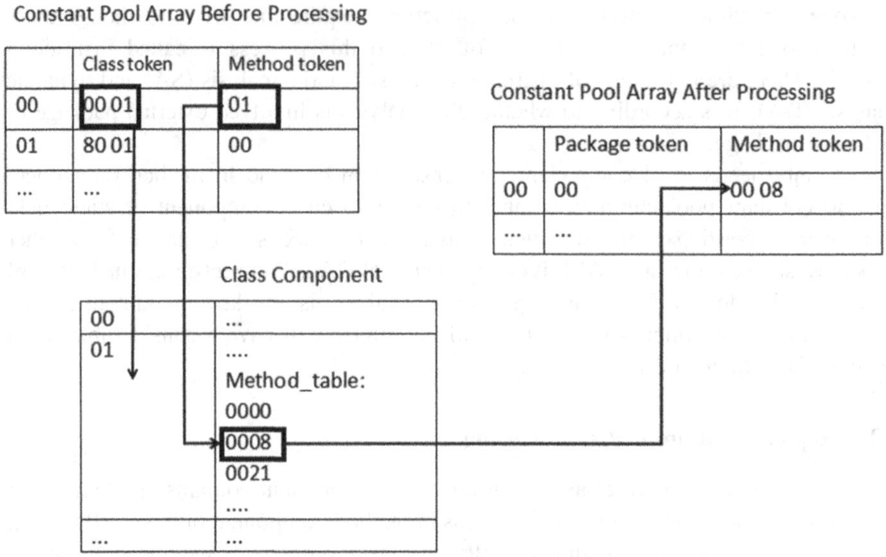

Constant Pool Array Before Processing

| | Class token | Method token |
|---|---|---|
| 00 | 00 01 | 01 |
| 01 | 80 01 | 00 |
| ... | ... | |

Constant Pool Array After Processing

| | Package token | Method token |
|---|---|---|
| 00 | 00 | 00 08 |
| ... | ... | |

Class Component

| 00 | ... |
|---|---|
| 01 | .... |
| | Method_table:<br>0000<br>0008<br>0021<br>.... |
| ... | ... |

**Fig. 4.** Overview of the off-card pre-processing operation

Without pre-processing, bytecode in method component should reference to several component to get required information. Every time when JCVM accesses a component, it needs several times memory reading from EEPROM. After pre-processing, bytecode in method component can only reference to constant pool component to get a direct offset to method, class or field. Thus pre-processing can increase executing rate by reducing number of accessing memory.

**On-card DA Implementation.** On-card DA is performed right after install CAP file onto card. The process is showed as below.

1. When executing an instruction we use its operand as a reference to constant pool array and will get a 4-byte information cp. The first byte $cp_0$ is also a tag identified this item. For example it is an item for external method.
2. Then the second byte $cp_1$ is a package token that the highest bit is 1 and the rest 7 bits as an index in import component. In the import component we can find the external package AID with the package token $cp_1$.
3. Through this AID and applet register table stored in memory, we can get the address of that external package. We need information of its export component.
4. We use $cp_2$, a class token, as an index to export component to get the external class offset.
5. Find class in external applet class component with class offset and use $cp_3$, a method token, to find the offset of method.
6. Referred to method component, get the address of this method and replace into constant pool array.

Figure 5 takes method invoke operation as example to show the process of DA.

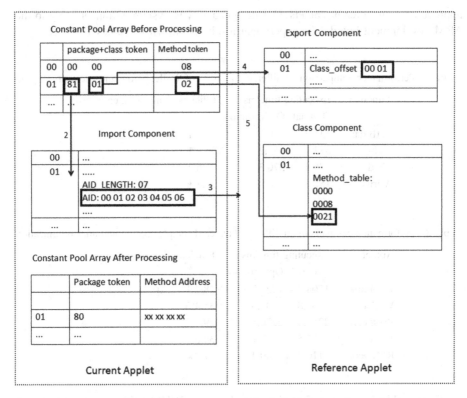

**Fig. 5.** Overview of the on-card pre-processing operation

In Fig. 5 shows the operation from step 2 to step 5. It is a time-consuming process if it is analyzed in JCVM when executing instruction. The dynamic pre-processing will have an amazing performance if the applet has a great number of external package invoking, or when circularly call the same external method. The pre-processing method makes constant pool array expanded from 4 byte to 6 byte, but considering the improvement to execution rate, this overhead can be accepted.

## 4 Experiment Result

In this paper, we proposed an implementation of the interpreter in JCVM and an optimization that exploited off-card/on-card co-design pre-processing method to CAP file such that it can reduce the time for the instruction analysis and raise the whole execution rate. In this section we report the experiment result regarding different Java card applets that we took into consideration. To verify the efficiency improvement of the proposed design, we conduct two experiments. First running different functions of Wallet on JCVM and comparing execution time before and after system optimization. Next several typical Java card applets are selected to execute on our designed JCVM with the optimization method proposed and to compare the difference of efficiency improvement on different applets. Our designed JCVM system is transplanting to the ARM development board. The experiment result are shown in Tables 1 and 2.

**Table 1.** Performance comparison on different functions of Wallet before and after optimization

| Function | Executing time/ms | | Efficiency improvement/% |
|---|---|---|---|
| | Original | Optimization | |
| getBalance | 131.2 | 80.1 | 38.9% |
| Debit | 573.1 | 362.2 | 36.9% |
| Credit | 575.4 | 370.3 | 35.6% |
| Verify | 152.1 | 100.8 | 33.7% |

**Table 2.** Performance comparison on different Java card samples before and after optimization

| Applet | Executing time/ms | | Efficiency improvement/% |
|---|---|---|---|
| | Original | Optimization | |
| JavaPurse | 1704.2 | 1223.3 | 28.2% |
| Wallet | 367.8 | 237.6 | 35.4% |
| Photocard | 3230.3 | 2276.5 | 29.5% |
| JavaLoyalty | 61.5 | 40.1 | 34.8% |
| RMIDemo | 110.2 | 80.4 | 27.0% |

From Table 1, we can find that the designed JCVM with the pre-processing approach presents an overall time reduction of 36.3% compared to the design without optimization. In Table 2 as well, the Java card efficiency improvement reaches 30.9% average.

## 5    Conclusion

The response time is one of the key criterion for Java card. The research we carried out in this paper is about JCVM, a key component in Java card relevant to applets executed. In this paper, we presented the design architecture of JCVM and the implementation of each module. The proposed optimization method combined an off-card static analysis and an on-card dynamic analysis to speed up the execution rate of JCVM. The pre-processing of CAP file is separated from the instruction interpreting process thus it can have a considerable improvement since it has reduced the time in interpreting. The experiment result demonstrated that the pre-processing method can gain an improvement on efficiency of 36.3%.

**Acknowledgments.** The research was supported by the National Natural Science Foundation of China (No. 61402546). The project has also been supported by two Technology Projects of Guangzhou (No. 201604016126) and (No. 201604010110).

# References

1. Oracle, Java Card 3 Platform: Runtime Environment Specification, Classic Edition. Version 3.0.4. Oracle, September 2011
2. Oracle, Java Card 3 Platform: Virtual Machine Specification, Classic Edition. Version 3.0.4. Oracle, September 2011
3. Oracle, Java Card 3 Platform: Application Programming Interface Specification, Classic Edition. Version 3.0.4. Oracle, September 2011
4. Chen, Z.: Java Card™ Technology for Smart Cards. Java Card Technology for Smart Cards: Architecture and Programmer's Guide. Addison-Wesley Longman Publishing Co. Inc (2000)
5. Ertl, M.A.: Threaded code variations and optimizations. In: EuroForth 2001 Conference Proceedings, pp. 49–55 (2001)
6. Gregg, D., Ertl, M.A., Krall, A.: A fast Java interpreter. In: Proceedings of the Workshop on Java Optimization Strategies for Embedded Systems (JOSES), Citeseer, Genoa (2001)
7. Jin, M.-S., Choi, W.-H., Yang, Y.-S., Jung, M.-S.: A study on fast JCVM with new transaction mechanism and caching-buffer based on Java card objects with a high locality. In: Enokido, T., Yan, L., Xiao, B., Kim, D., Dai, Y., Yang, Laurence T. (eds.) EUC 2005. LNCS, vol. 3823, pp. 91–100. Springer, Heidelberg (2005). https://doi.org/10.1007/11596042_10
8. Zilli, M., Raschke, W., Weiss, R., et al.: Hardware/software co-design for a high-performance Java card interpreter in low-end embedded systems. Microprocess. Microsyst. 39(8), 1076–1086 (2015)
9. Liu, T., Zhang, D., Jiang, Y.: Research and Implementation of Bytecode Instruction Folding on Java Card (2014)
10. Cao, X., Ying, L.I.: Feedback-based JCVM instruction prescheduling scheme. Comput. Eng. 40(1), 78–82 (2014)

# ACCDSE: A Design Space Exploration Framework for Convolutional Neural Network Accelerator

Zhisheng Li[1(✉)], Lei Wang[1], Qiang Dou[1], Yuxing Tang[1], Shasha Guo[1], Haifang Zhou[1], and Wenyuan Lu[2]

[1] National University of Defense Technology, Changsha, China
lizhsh_123@163.com
[2] Xi'an Satellite Monitoring and Control Center, Xi'an, China

**Abstract.** In deep learning, convolutional neural network (CNN) is quite representative. The convolutional operation of CNN is the focus of hardware acceleration research. Because of CNN's memory-intensive and compute-intensive features, increasing size of network poses a greater challenge on the design of the hardware accelerator. We need to determine the parameters of the accelerator at the early stages of the accelerator design.

This paper presents a design space exploration framework for CNN accelerator: ACCDSE, for determining the parameters of convolutional accelerator in FPGA. Simulation method and theoritical computation method are both used to find the optimal parameter. Experiment on LeNet shows that 16-bit fixed point is the most economical data precision for inference of LeNet. By theoritical analysis, the ACCDSE framework can obtain optimal matrix tiling parameters. Without decreasing the classification accuracy, the power consumption can be reduced by 33.57% and the storage can be reduced by 41.47% after weight pruning.

**Keywords:** CNN · Design space exploration · Data precision
Accelerator · Weight pruning

## 1 Introduction

In recent years, deep learning has subverted the algorithm design ideas in many areas, such as speech recognition and image classification. Since AlexNet wons the 2012 ImageNet large-scale image recognition competition (ILSVRC2012) with 83.6% top-5 accuracy, CNNs have become well-known. Nowadays, artificial intelligence is commonly applied to industrial manufacture. Because CNN's convolutional layers have a significant effect in extracting image features, CNN is widely used in practical applications. It makes the requirements for CNN's inference phase are increasing. However, CNN has the property of memory-intensive and compute-intensive. In addition, the scale of CNN continues to increase. These two facts make the hardware acceleration for CNN a urgent issue. Since

W. Xu et al. (Eds.): NCCET 2017, CCIS 600, pp. 22–34, 2018.
https://doi.org/10.1007/978-981-10-7844-6_3

the convolutional layers of CNN takes about 90% of the execution time [11], it is the focus of hardware acceleration. At present, there are a lot of accelerations for CNN. GPU, FPGA [10,13,16] and ASIC [3] are commonly used acceleration platform.

To meet various design target, accelerator design parameters need to be determined at early stages. Many aspects of CNN optimization and acceleration need to be considered, such as the design of the architecture [14], the parameter for matrix tiling [10,13,16], whether or not using low-precision operands [6].

However, previous research work focuses on a single aspect parameter setting. But these parameters are interactional and accelerator design is a system design process. In order to receive more systematic solution, we need a design space exploration framework to find the best parameters combination according to performance requirements.

This paper presents a design space exploration framework: ACCDSE. This framework is based on a in-house simulator that supports CNN's inference and three design space exploration modules. The three modules can find optimal configuration parameters that meet the performance requirements for data precision, matrix tiling, and weight pruning, respectively. The main contributions of this paper are as follows:

1. Proposed a design space exploration framework that supports CNN's inference engine's DSE;
2. Explored the impact of various data precision on the accuracy of prediction, selecting the most economical data precision;
3. Based on the roofline model and the matrix tiling strategy, the parallel parameters are selected under the given hardware constraint;
4. Explored the relationship among classification accuracy, power and weight pruning.

Through experiment with LeNet and Caffe's performance as benchmark, the design space exploration result shows that 16-bit fixed point operand data precision will not have an impact on performance. The matrix tiling module in the framework can calculate the optimal parameter configuration according to the convolutional layer parameters and the resource limit of the acceleration platform to achieve the maximum throughput. Without decreasing the classification performance priority, the storage can be reduced by 33.57% after weight pruning. When we concerned more about power, classification accuracy decreases by 4.0%, the storage can be reduced by 78.03% after weight pruning. If we concerned more about cost, the storage can be reduced by 49.89% after weight pruning without sacrificing classification accuracy.

The rest of this paper is organized as follows: The Sect. 2 introduces the background and the related research work. The Sect. 3 analyzes the parallel characteristics of the convolutional operation. The Sect. 4 introduces the proposed ACCDSE in this paper. The Sect. 5, shows the experiments and performance analysis. The Sect. 6 is the work related to this research. The Sect. 7 is the conclusion.

**Table 1.** LeNet parameters

| LeNet parameters | | | | |
|---|---|---|---|---|
| Layer type | Input | Weights | Stride | Output |
| CONV1 | 1*28*28 | 20*1*5*5 | 1 | 20*24*24 |
| Pooling1 | 20*24*24 | | 2 | 20*12*12 |
| CONV2 | 20*12*12 | 50*20*5*5 | 1 | 50*8*8 |
| Pooling2 | 50*8*8 | | 2 | 50*4*4 |
| FC1 | 800*1 | 800*500 | | 500*1 |
| ReLU | 500*1 | | | 500*1 |
| FC2 | 500*1 | 500*10 | | 10*1 |
| Soft-Max | 10*1 | | | 10*1 |

## 2  Background

There are many algorithms for convolutional neural networks, but the main components are the same. In this paper, we use LeNet as a research neural network.

### 2.1  LeNet

LeNet is the most basic network of CNN, mainly used in handwritten number recognition. As is shown in Fig. 1, it is divided into eight layers, including tow convolutional layers, two pooling layers, two fully-connected layers, one ReLU layer and one SoftMax layer [6]. The Table 1 shows the parameter for the LeNet.

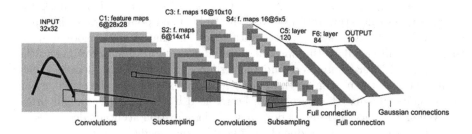

**Fig. 1.** LeNet structure

### 2.2  Convolutional Operation

As is shown in Fig. 2, the convolutional operation is the point product of a three-dimensional matrix and a four-dimensional matrix. In the process of operation, the convolutional kernel performs the point product in the order of the corresponding data of the input matrix, the result is summed to obtain a point of the

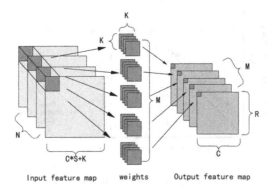

**Fig. 2.** Convolutional layer diagram

output matrix finally. Different groups of convolutional kernel repeat the same operation. When all the kernels and the input matrix complete the operation after the corresponding output matrix, a convolutional operation is completed. Figure 4 shows the pseudo-code of the convolutional operation.

### 2.3    Roofline Model

Using the FPGA platform to accelerate the CNN, two major problems need to be solved. First, improve the utilization of resources. Second, meet the FPGA bandwidth requirements [16]. In order to solve these two problems, this paper takes the Roofline Model [9].

Figure 3 shows the Roofline Model. As is shown in the figure, the slash represents the bandwidth of the platform. The line paralleled to the X axis represents the resource limit of the platform. It can be seen that the area among the slash, the line and the X axis is achievable. For point in the slash above, the limiting factor is the bandwidth. For point in the straight line above, the limiting factor is the resources. Two algorithms are shown in the figure. Obviously, in Fig. 3 the throughput of algorithm 1 is smaller than that of algorithm 2. When the throughput is the same, the computation to communication ratio (CTC) high point's performance is better [16].

## 3    Convolutional Operation Parallelism Analysis

As is shown in Fig. 4(a), the convolutional operation is a multiple nested loop. The same loop internal data is independent of each other and can be executed in parallel. The research of this paper is mainly for the following three parallel characteristics.

As is shown in Fig. 4(a), the 5th and 6th loop represent the convolutional kernel. The data inside the convolutional kernel is independent of each other and can be executed in parallel. We denote $Tk$ as the number of data, which within the same convolutional kernel, executed at the same time ($Tk <= K * K$).

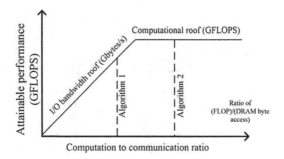

**Fig. 3.** Roofline model

```
for (r=0;r<R;r++){
 for (c=0;c<C;c++){
  for (m=0;m<M;m++){
   for (n=0;n<N;n++){
    for (i=0;i<K;i++){
     for (j=0;j<K;j++){
      output[m][r][c]+=
      weights[m][n][i][j]*input[n][S*r+i][S*c+j];
}}}}}}
```

```
for (r=0;r<R;r++){
 for (c=0;c<C;c++){
  for (m=0;m<min(M,m+Tm);m+=Tm){
  #Tile Tm times
   for (n=0;n<min(N,n+Tn);n+=Tn){
   #Tile Tn times
    for (i=0;i<min(K*K,i+Tk);i+=Tk){
    #Tile Tk times
     x=i/K;y=i%K;
     output[m][r][c]+=
     weights[m][n][x][y]*input[n][S*r+x][S*c+y];
}}}}}
```

(a) Pseudo code of a convolutional layer (b) Pseudo code of a tiled convolutional layer

**Fig. 4.** Convolutional pseudocode

The 4th loop represents the data between the convolutional kernels. The data between the convolutional kernels are independent of each other and can be executed in parallel. We denote $Tn$ as the number of convolutional kernel executed at the same time $(Tn <= N)$.

Similarly, the 3th loop is among the different outputs. The data are also independent of each other, which can be executed in parallel. We denote $Tm$ as the number of output executed at the same time $(Tm <= M)$.

The convolutional code for adding the parallel parameters is shown in Fig. 4(b).

The matrix tiling calculation model is based on the method of work [10, 16]. Figure 2 shows the meaning of the relevant parameters. The Eq. (1) shows the number of cycles for the convolutional layer:

$$
\begin{aligned}
number \quad of \quad execution \quad cycle = \\
\left\lceil \frac{M}{Tm} \right\rceil \times \left\lceil \frac{N}{Tn} \right\rceil \times \left\lceil \frac{RC}{TrTc} \right\rceil \times \left\lceil \frac{K}{Ti} \right\rceil \times \left\lceil \frac{K}{Tj} \right\rceil \times \left( TrTc \times \left\lceil \frac{TiTj}{Tk} \right\rceil + P \right)
\end{aligned}
\tag{1}
$$

Where P is the number of pipelines, Tr, Tc, Ti, and Tj are the dimensions of the data to be prepared in one operation. The total number of operations for calculating a convolutional layer is shown in Eq. (2):

$$
total \quad number \quad of \quad operations = 2 \times R \times C \times M \times N \times K \times K
\tag{2}
$$

Equation (3) represents the upper limit of the calculation under parallel parameters:

$$computational \quad roof = $$
$$\frac{2 \times M \times N \times K \times K}{\left\lceil \frac{M}{Tm} \right\rceil \times \left\lceil \frac{N}{Tn} \right\rceil \times \left\lceil \frac{K}{Ti} \right\rceil \times \left\lceil \frac{K}{Tj} \right\rceil \times \left\lceil \frac{TiTj}{Tk} \right\rceil} \tag{3}$$

The purpose of optimizing acceleration is to maximize the computational roof.

All operations are required for data support. The amount of data set must be less than the bandwidth of the platform.

The data involved in the operation is divided into three parts: input, weights and output. Hence, different buffer are required to hold the necessary data. The data required for the three-part data are shown in (4) (5) (6):

$$\beta_{in} = Tn \times (S \times Tr + Ti - S)(S \times Tc + Tj - S) \times 2\,Bytes \tag{4}$$

$$\beta_{weights} = Tm \times Tn \times Ti \times Tj \times 2\,Bytes \tag{5}$$

$$\beta_{out} = Tm \times Tr \times Tc \times 2\,Bytes \tag{6}$$

Similarly, the number of loads and stores can be calculated using (7) (8) (9):

$$\alpha_{in} = \frac{M}{Tm} \times \frac{N}{Tn} \times \frac{R}{Tr} \times \frac{C}{Tc} \times \frac{K}{Ti} \times \frac{K}{Tj} \tag{7}$$

$$\alpha_{weights} = \frac{M}{Tm} \times \frac{N}{Tn} \times \frac{R}{Tr} \times \frac{C}{Tc} \times \frac{K}{Ti} \times \frac{K}{Tj} \tag{8}$$

$$\alpha_{out} = 2 \times M \times R \times C \tag{9}$$

The amount of memory and the buffer size can be calculated by calculating the communication ratio. Calculating the communication ratio is a measure of the degree of reuse of the on-chip storage data.

$$CTC = \frac{Total \quad required \quad computation}{Total \quad requried \quad communication}$$
$$= \frac{2 \times M \times N \times R \times C \times K \times K}{\alpha_{in} \times \beta_{in} + \alpha_{weights} \times \beta_{weights}\alpha_{out} \times \beta_{out}} \tag{10}$$

CTC as the horizontal axis, the throughput of the vertical axis, all the circumstances listed. According to rooflin model theory, we select the highest throughput point as the design point.

## 4    ACCDSE Framework

The objective of this paper is to determine the parameters of the design space exploration based on the metric such as performance, power and energy efficiency, so that the accelerator can meet the design requirements. Figure 5 shows the framework for design space exploration. The design parameters that can be selected in this framework, including the data precision, the parameters of matrix tiling and whether or not performing the pruning operation.

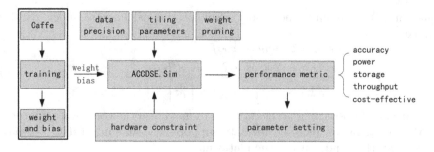

**Fig. 5.** Design space exploration framework

## 4.1  Data Precision Selection

High data precision can lead to stable performance. Low data precision will save hardware costs. Appropriate data precision is a trade-off between performance and hardware costs.

Weights of trained Caffe Model are extracted and fed into the simulator. We observed that the absolute value of the extracted weights is between 0 and 1. Through the method of enlarging the data, we convert float point data to fixed point data. The data after processing is involved in the operation. The result of the calculation needs to be reduced to the original size. In the process of operation, inappropriate data precision may lead to data overflow. The data overflow will cause the result of inference to be invalid. There are three data precisions in the framework: float point, 32-bit fixed point and 16-bit fixed point. Through the experimental analysis, we select the most suitable data precision.

## 4.2  Matrix Tiling Parameters

In Sect. 3, three parallel parameters $(Tk, Tn, Tm)$ have been proposed. In the process of hardware acceleration, the utilization of hardware resources and bandwidth must be considered. Inappropriate parallel parameters, always leading to reduction in resource utilization, and failing to achieve good performance.
The choice of parallel parameters must follow three principles:

(1) the design of the buffers size must not exceed the on-chip memory,
(2) the design of the bandwidth must not exceed the maximum bandwidth,
(3) the computing unit must not exceed the on-chip resources.

In this calculation module, entering the resource constraint and convolutional layer parameters, the output is matrix tiling parameters.
As the work in [16], there are 3 steps to select parameters.

(1) According to resource constraints, the theoretical maximum throughput is obtained.
(2) According to the convolutional layer parameters and Roofline Model calculated computational roof and CTC.

(3) After listing all possible parameter configurations, we select the best point as the design point.

Assuming our implementation is built on the VC707 board which has a Xilinx FPGA chip Virtex7 485t, we optimize CONV2 which in Table 1. The data precision is 16-bit fixed point. By calculation, the theoretical maximum throughput is 140 GFLOPS. By calculating the model, CTC and computational roof are obtained. With the bandwidth limit, the maximum throughput point is the design point. At this time the parameters $(Tk, Tm, Tn)$ are $(25, 5, 5)$. At this point, the throughput is 125 GOPS.

### 4.3   Weight Pruning

In the work [12], the contribution of different weights to the final prediction results is different. A small part of the weight can determine the final performance. In the process of optimizing the CNN, the weight that makes a great contribution to the result, is preserved. The weight that has smaller contribution is selectively removed. Through the pruning operation, power and storage can be reduced at the same time, and meanwhile having no significant impact on performance.

The strategy in this framework is to set a value appropriate threshold. The weight which does not exceed the threshold, will be set to zero. Threshold size of the selection, can only affect little to final results, but also as much as possible to reduce the amount of computing, power and storage. It can be found that a suitable threshold is critical to optimization.

## 5   Experimental Evaluation

### 5.1   Experimental Environment

Caffe is the classical framework of convolutional neural networks. In this paper we use Caffe as the training framework and inference reference model. Caffe trained the LeNet network with the MNIST training set. The weight of the simulator comes from the trained Caffe Model. Caffe's output is used as the baseline. The ACCDSE framework is running on ubuntu 16.04 system. The processor is Intel Core i5-6600.

### 5.2   Implementation

The ACCDSE framework proposed in this paper is implemented in C. The key component of the ACCDSE framework is a CNN inference engine simulator. Figure 6 presents the structure of the ACCDSE framework implementation. Caffe uses the training set in MNIST to train and get the weights. The simulator that obtained the weight is evaluated with the MNIST test set. The results are compared with Caffe's test performance and analysis. The simulator can perform data precision, matrix tiling and weight pruning selection. As mentioned in the

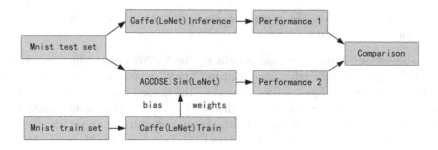

**Fig. 6.** Diagram of the experimental process

Sect. 4, the options for selecting data precision are float point, 16-bit fixed point and 32-bit fixed point. Matrix tiling with $(Tk, Tm, Tn)$ three parameters. Weight pruning has a choice of thresholds.

### 5.3   Experimental Result

### 5.3.1   Data Precision

Our simulator can select the data precision. In Sect. 4, we have proposed a method of data type selection. Caffe's classification accuracy as the baseline. 10,000 pictures of Mnist test set as benchmark. Float point, 32-bit fixed point and 16-bit fixed point three data precision experiment for performance comparison respectively. By using the Sect. 4.1's method, we transform the weight into fixed point. The middle value is saved with double bit width. When the median value participates in the next operation, the value is scaled and rounding. When the number of significant digits is 1 and the error rate is high, there is no representation in the figure. The overflow situation is also not shown in the figure.

First, the simulator analyzes the weights (absolute value), and the weight distribution is shown in Fig. 7. The results show that the weights are mostly between 0.01 and 0.1. So, when the weights are converted to integers and magnified by a factor of 1,000, the vast majority of the weights are covered.

The experimental results are shown in Fig. 8. The horizontal axis is the data precision, and the number of significant digits of the weight is marked in parentheses. The red dotted line indicates the performance of Caffe.

Through the experimental results, high data precision will lead to stable performance (compare with baseline) and not easy to overflow. When the data precision is 16-bit fixed point and 32-bit fixed point, the more the effective bit of the weight, the better the performance. According to the comparison among all of the performances of data under precision, int and 16-bit fixed point have the best performance, which is better than baseline. At this time, the weight of the amplification parameter of 1000, confirms the conclusions of Fig. 7. The principle of selecting data precision: performance priority, hardware costs secondly. According to the principle, we select 16-bit fixed point as the data precision.

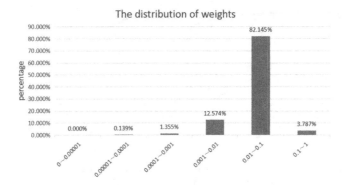

**Fig. 7.** The distribution of weights (absolute value)

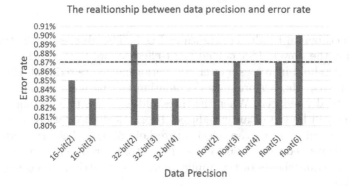

**Fig. 8.** Performance under three data precision (Color figure online)

### 5.3.2   Weight Pruning

The simulator can research the relationship among threshold, calculation and accuracy. The steps are as follows. When the simulator reads the weights, the total number of weights and the number of pruning are counted. When the parameters of the convolutional layer are determined, the total amount can be calculated according to the parameters. Similarly, according to the number of pruning weights, we can also get the amount of weight after the calculation. Here, we calculate the amount as a criterion for power consumption. The experiment was conducted with the MNIST 10000 test set as a benchmark. The experiment uses 16-bit fixed point as the data precision.

We denote P as the number of correct samples, P' as the total number of samples, M as the storage after the pruning of the weights, M' as the storage before pruning, Q as the calculated amount after the pruning of the weights, Q' as the amount of computation before pruning, E as the power efficiency, and C as the cost-effective.

The relationship shown as follows: $accuracy = P/P'$, $storage = M/M'$, $power = Q/Q'$, $E = P/Q$, $C = E/(1 - accuracy)$.

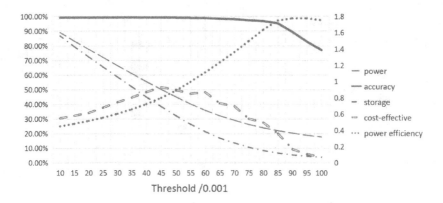

**Fig. 9.** The relationship between threshold and performance index

The experimental results are shown in Fig. 9. The abscissa is the threshold. In the figure, the power efficiency and cost-effective are the trend lines.

As the threshold increases, power and performance are reduced. However, in a particular area, the performance degradation can be ignored, but the power will be drastically reduced. When the threshold increases to a certain value, the performance will be significantly reduced. If practical applications is concerned about the performance, we can select a threshold of 0.03. The error rate is only 0.81%, the power reduced to 66.43%, and the storage reduced to 58.57%. If the performance requirements of the application are very strict, we do not have to take pruning.

If the actual application is more concerned about power, we select the highest power efficiency point. When the threshold is 0.09, the power efficiency is the highest. But at this time, the error rate is 10%. The performance is unbearable obviously. The final selection threshold is 0.085 as the design point. At this time, the error rate is 4.86%, the power is only 21.97%, the storage reduced to 6.58%.

If the actual application is more concerned about the cost-effective, we can select threshold of 0.045, which is the best cost-effective point obviously. In this time, power and performance achieve the best match. At this point, the error rate is 0.84%, the storage reduced to 38.42%, and the power reduced to 50.11%.

## 6    Related Work

CNN accelerator design work has been carried out for several years. ASIC, FPGA and GPU are the main acceleration platforms. Among them the most famous ASIC is DianNao series of accelerators. Work [3] introduced the first accelerator. The acceleration strategy is to separate the operations in the network, then calculate each neuron, finally get the results. The nearest accelerator is ShiDianDao [4]. Obtaining the data in the terminal directly, this could avoid some of the memory consumption. In addition, IBM developed the TureNorth chip [1]. The data is transmitted using spiking. The advantages of FPGAs are flexibility and low power consumption. The acceleration work is mainly applied to the inference. GPU is generally used for training.

In the chip design, the key problem is solving resources and bandwidth, so design space exploration is very important. In work [10,16], the Roofline Model is used to solve the problem of resource and bandwidth in FPGA. In view of the problem of resource utilization is not well, the work [13], put forward the idea of hardware resource block, making the use of resources more fine-grained. There is still a lot of work designed for the computing unit. For example, the work [5,14]. In addition, work [12] is referred to the weight pruning operation. This is also the future direction of CNN accelerator design. The corresponding work [7] proposed an effective compression engine. In work [6], we study the problem of finite numerical precision, and also provide a very bright direction for the acceleration work. Work [15] also design and implement Caffeine, a hardware/software co-designed library to efficiently accelerate the entire CNN on FPGAs.

The method proposed in work [2] uses the data correlation among the multi-layer convolutional layers to improve the data reuse and reduce the pressure of the bandwidth. In work [8], the neural network compilation method is proposed, which can match the network and hardware.

## 7  Conclusion

This paper presents ACCDSE, a design space exploration framework for convolutional neural network accelerator. Taking LeNet as an example, the FPGA is used to accelerate the platform. The framework has been used for data precision, matrix tiling and weight pruning selection.

Experiment result shows that ACCDSE can achieve the most economical precision selection for convolutional neural network to achieve maximum throughput. It can make full use of the acceleration platform hardware resources. The weight pruning enables a combination of power and performance. Through this framework optimization, the accelerator can achieve trade-offs among throughput, performance, and power. Under a variety of performance requirements, the accelerator can achieve optimal parameter configuration.

**Acknowledgment.** This project was supported by NSFC 61402501. I was also grateful to my teachers and students who had helped me in this project.

## References

1. Akopyan, F., Sawada, J., Cassidy, A., Alvarez-Icaza, R.: Truenorth: design and tool flow of a 65 mw 1 million neuron programmable neurosynaptic chip. IEEE Trans. Comput. Aided Des. Integr. Circ. Syst. **34**(10), 1537–1557 (2015)
2. Alwani, M., Chen, H., Ferdman, M., Milder, P.: Fused-layer CNN accelerators. In: 2016 49th Annual IEEE/ACM International Symposium on Microarchitecture (MICRO), pp. 1–12, October 2016

3. Chen, T., Du, Z., Sun, N., Wang, J., Wu, C., Chen, Y., Temam, O.: Diannao: a small-footprint high-throughput accelerator for ubiquitous machine-learning. In: International Conference on Architectural Support for Programming Languages and Operating Systems, pp. 269–284 (2014)

4. Du, Z., Fasthuber, R., Chen, T., Ienne, P., Li, L., Luo, T., Feng, X., Chen, Y., Temam, O.: Shidiannao: shifting vision processing closer to the sensor. In: Proceedings of the International Symposium on Computer Architecture, ISCA 2015, pp. 92–104 (2015)

5. Farabet, C., Poulet, C., Han, J.Y., Lecun, Y.: CNP: an FPGA-based processor for convolutional networks. In: International Conference on Field Programmable Logic and Applications, pp. 32–37 (2009)

6. Gupta, S., Agrawal, A., Gopalakrishnan, K., Narayanan, P.: Deep learning with limited numerical precision. Computer Science (2015)

7. Han, S., Liu, X., Mao, H., Pu, J., Pedram, A., Horowitz, M.A., Dally, W.J.: EIE: efficient inference engine on compressed deep neural network. In: International Symposium on Computer Architecture, pp. 243–254 (2016)

8. Ji, Y., Zhang, Y.H., Li, S.C., Chi, P., Jiang, C.H., Qu, P., Xie, Y., Chen, W.G.: Neutrams: neural network transformation and co-design under neuromorphic hardware constraints. In: The IEEE/ACM International Symposium on Microarchitecture, pp. 1–13 (2016)

9. Meloni, P., Deriu, G., Conti, F., Loi, I., Raffo, L., Benini, L.: Curbing the roofline: a scalable and flexible architecture for CNNS on FPGA. In: The ACM International Conference, pp. 376–383 (2016)

10. Motamedi, M., Gysel, P., Akella, V., Ghiasi, S.: Design space exploration of FPGA-based deep convolutional neural networks. In: Asia and South Pacific Design Automation Conference, pp. 575–580 (2016)

11. Peemen, M., Setio, A., Mesman, B., Corporaal, H.: Memory-centric accelerator design for Convolutional Neural Networks (2013)

12. Reagen, B., Whatmough, P., Adolf, R., Rama, S., Lee, H., Lee, S.K., Jos Ndez-Lobato, M., Wei, G.Y., Brooks, D.: Minerva: enabling low-power, highly-accurate deep neural network accelerators. In: ACM/IEEE International Symposium on Computer Architecture, pp. 267–278 (2016)

13. Shen, Y., Ferdman, M., Milder, P.: Overcoming resource underutilization in spatial CNN accelerators (2016)

14. Wang, C., Gong, L., Yu, Q., Li, X.: DLAU: a scalable deep learning accelerator unit on FPGA (2016)

15. Zhang, C., Fang, Z., Zhou, P., Pan, P., Cong, J.: Caffeine: towards uniformed representation and acceleration for deep convolutional neural networks. In: International Conference on Computer Aided Design (2016)

16. Zhang, C., Li, P., Sun, G., Guan, Y., Xiao, B., Cong, J.: Optimizing FPGA-based accelerator design for deep convolutional neural networks. In: ACM/SIGDA International Symposium on Field-Programmable Gate Arrays, pp. 161–170 (2015)

# A Programmable Pre-emphasis Transmitter for SerDes in 40 nm CMOS

Hongbing Tan, Haiyan Chen, Sheng Liu$^{(\boxtimes)}$, Xikun Ma, and Yaqing Chi

School of National University of Defense Technology,
Changsha 410073, Hunan, People's Republic of China
tanhongbing1993@163.com, hychen608@163.com, liusheng83@163.com,
xkma503@163.com, yqchi@163.com

**Abstract.** Based on 40 nm standard CMOS process, this paper proposes an easy realized, programmable pre-emphasis transmitter. The circuit is used in high performance SerDes (Serializer-Deserializer) chip, which utilizes a 2-tap current-mode pre-emphasis technique, resulting less design complicacy as well as low noise. Furthermore, a tail current DAC enables equalization to be configurable in order to adapt to various data rate condition. Simulation results show 0–6 db pre-emphasis ability and 0–1.3 V differential output voltage swing under 2.5–6.25 GB/s transmission rate, which meet specifications of high speed serial link standards such as PCIE2.1 and RapidIO2.2.

**Keywords:** Current-mode driver · Feed forward equalization
SerDes · Programmable pre-emphasis

## 1 Introduction

The demand of bandwidth for the transmission has increased a lot with the rapidly development of integrated circuit, which caused interface bandwidth become a bottleneck for performance improvement in digital systems [1]. Traditional parallel interface need more chip pins to provide enough bandwidth but its signal attenuation also become a serious problem while data rate beyond 1 Gbps [8]. However, high-speed serial link which based on SerDes (Serializer, De-serializer) can work at dozens of Gbps and consume less energy [3], such as PCIE and RapidIO, which attract many researchers interest. SerDes chips adopt analog and digital circuit mixed design technology to resolve signal integrality problems such as channel attenuation and Inter Symbol Interference (ISI)[10].

Transmitter is an important part in SerDes which consume a large percentage of serial-link power. Most transmitters adopt 2-tap pre-emphasis that data code and pre-emphasis code combine with voltage or current mode to form a pre-emphasis driver. Young-Hoon song and Samuel Palermo designed a voltage-mode transmitter with current-mode equalization in 90-nm CMOS baud rate achieving 6 Gbps [6], which makes full use of current mode pre-emphasis and low power consumption characteristics. Huang proposed a 80 mw 40 GB/s transmitter with automatic serializing time window search and 2-tap pre-emphasis

© Springer Nature Singapore Pte Ltd. 2018
W. Xu et al. (Eds.): NCCET 2017, CCIS 600, pp. 35–44, 2018.
https://doi.org/10.1007/978-981-10-7844-6_4

in 65 nm CMOS technology [4], but it is not programmable. This paper proposes a programmable pre-emphasis transmitter for SerDes, which not only realizes traditional function of driver circuit, but also adds extensibility and programmable ability with little complexity. This transmitter realize programmable pre-emphasis and output amplitude based on 40 nm COMS process. Moreover, it can work in different channel conditions at 2.5–6.25 GB/s transmission rate, and satisfying variety of standard protocols.

The paper is organized as follows: Sect. 2 explains the pre-emphasis technique and the overall architecture of the SerDes. The circuit design of functional blocks is described in Sect. 3. Section 4 shows the implementation and simulation results. Finally, a conclusion is made in Sect. 5.

## 2    Pre-emphasis Technique

An ideal rectangular wave can be decomposed into different frequency cosine harmonic [7], and the attenuation always occurs on high frequency due to the low pass characteristics of transmission channel. Moreover, the high frequency components mainly affect the signal jump edge, so compensating attenuation means compensating signal jump edge, i.e. pre-emphasis technique [5]. Figure 1 shows the pre-emphasis amplifies the high frequency components, which can offset emphasis and attenuation to obtain a smooth response [2].

The basic structure of the 2-tap pre-emphasis driver as shown in Fig. 2(a), *imain* and *ipos* are two tail currents Rt is a 50 Ω resistor network to match channel impedance, and *vptx* is supply voltage. The serializer provides differential bits *mainp/mainn* and pre-emphasis bits *pos1p/pos1n*, and combining them in form of current or voltage to realize pre-emphasis.

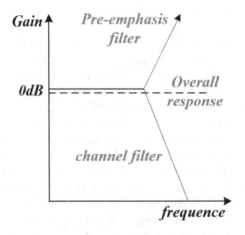

**Fig. 1.** The function of pre-emphasis

We list the voltages of *txp*, *txn* and their difference in Table 1, and the corresponding values of differential bits *MAIN* and pre-emphasis bits *POS1* are list in Fig. 2(b).

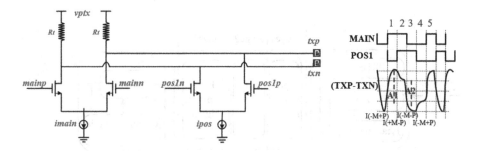

**Fig. 2.** Two-tap current mode pre-emphasis driver. (a) is the driver circuit, (b) is the input data code

**Table 1.** The output voltage of driver (Rt = 50 Ω)

| Tap | 1 | 2 | 3 | 4 |
|---|---|---|---|---|
| txp | vptx | vptx-ipos*Rt | Vptx-(imain+ipos)*Rt | Vptx-imain*Rt |
| txn | vptx-(imain+ipos)*Rt | vptx-imain*Rt | vptx | vptx-ipos*Rt |
| txp-txn | (imain+ipos)*Rt | (imain-ipos)*Rt | -(imain+ipos)*Rt | -(imain-ipos)*Rt |

According to the Table 1, the output differential swing A1 and the differential swing A2 (without emphasis) is:

$$A1 = txp - txn = (imain + ipmos) * Rt \tag{1}$$

$$A2 = (imain - ipmos) * Rt \tag{2}$$

The pre-emphasis gain is:

$$EQ(dB) = 20\log\frac{A_1}{A_2} = 20\log(1 + \frac{2ipos}{imain - ipos}) \tag{3}$$

When output swing A1, pre-emphasis gain and termination resistors Rt are fixed, the *imain* and *ipos* can be calculated base on (1) and (2):

$$imain = 0.5 * (1 + \frac{A2}{A1}) * \frac{A1}{Rt} \tag{4}$$

$$ipos = 0.5 * (1 - \frac{A2}{A1}) * \frac{A1}{Rt} \tag{5}$$

# 3    Circuit Design

The overall structure of the proposed transmitter is shown in Fig. 3, which consists of synchronization module, serializer and driver.

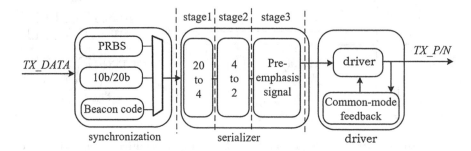

**Fig. 3.** The overall structure of transmitter

Synchronization module preprocesses the data which come from data link layer that transfer it into 20 bits. Then, choosing one in three base on the control bits, and the three choices include 20 bits parallel data, the output of PRBS generator, and Beacon code. This module can be realized by Verilog programming.

Serializer adopts multi-phase single-stage and single-phase multi-stage circuit to realize serialization, which can raise the clock frequency step by step and reduce this modules working at high frequency clock. 20 bits parallel data are serialized to 1 bit after three stage serialization in its correspond clock frequency.

The driver converts digital signal to analog signal and realizes pre-emphasis before signals are sent to the channel. The width of the final output waveform and swing are determined by driver when impedance is matched.

## 3.1    Serializer Circuit Design

The structure of serializer is shown in Fig. 4, serializer converts parallel data to serial bit through three stages. Firstly, the input parallel data (20 bits) are divided into four channels each is 5 bits, and then sent them into four identical 5:1 selectors respectively to obtain 4 bits parallel data. Secondly, the 4 bits data are divided into two groups: data_a/b and data_c/d, taking data_a/b as a example, let data_a and data_b align with the posedge and the negedge of the 5*ft clock respectively to obtain signal a/b. Then a/b are sent into 2:1 selector for the second serialization under the 5*ft clock (sa). The selector is static CMOS circuit, their signal processing obeys:

$$out = \overline{\overline{sa \bullet a} \bullet \overline{sb \bullet b}} = sa \bullet a + sb \bullet b \qquad (6)$$

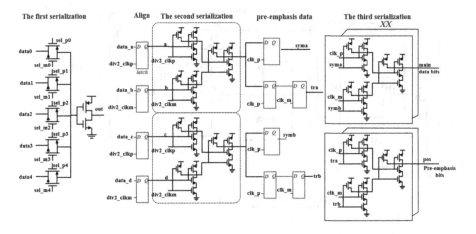

**Fig. 4.** The overall structure of transmitter

By the way, the pre-emphasis data obtained by utilizing a latch delay a clock cycle for the output data of the second serialization.

The third serialization realizes 2:1 conversion for the data bit and pre-emphasis bit using two selectors under the 10 ft clock. The structure of the selector is the same as the second serialization. In Fig. 4, XX means a number of parallel identical selectors, because multiple parallel selectors can increase the current and make the serialization work faster [9].

## 3.2   Pre-emphasis Programmable Design

According to Eq. (3), the effect of pre-emphasis can be expressed as:

$$EQ(dB) = 20 \log(1 + \frac{2}{\frac{\text{imain}}{\text{ipos}} - 1}) \tag{7}$$

In order to realize programmable pre-emphasis, i.e. programmable $ipos$, this paper design current steering DAC circuit is shown in Fig. 5, in which $iref$ is a reference current, tr_h[4:0] and tr_hn[4:0] are control bits, so $ipos$ is determined by:

$$ipos = \sum_{i=0}^{i=4} tr\_h[i] \bullet iref \tag{8}$$

Speed requirement is not strict to this DAC [11], because of current $ipos$ is fixed when control bits are configured. In this paper, in order to get an accurate and steady current, we adopt cascode source current.

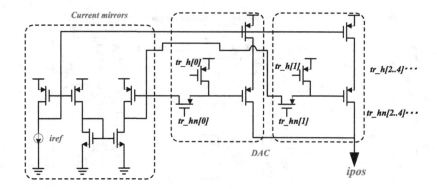

**Fig. 5.** Current tail DAC circuit

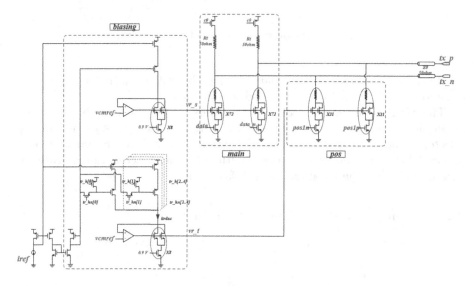

**Fig. 6.** The overall structure of transmitter

## 3.3   Driver Circuit Design

Figure 6 illustrates three modules of the driver in this paper, the biasing module produces current *imain* with the reference of current *iref*, the lower part is pre-emphasis programmable circuit which produces *ipos*. Main module and *pos* module are current mode driver.

When tr_h[4:0] = 10001 and Rt = 50 Ω, the result of simulation is shown in Fig. 7(a). The serial data baud rate is 5 GB/s and the pre-emphasis gain (EQ) is about 2 dB. Figure 7(b) shows indicate that there is liner correlation between tr_h[4:0] and EQ.

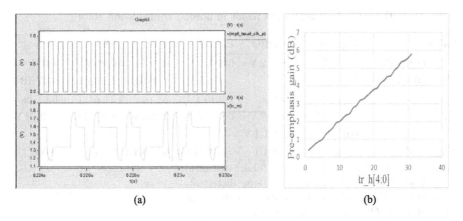

(a)                                    (b)

**Fig. 7.** The simulation results of pre-emphasis. (*a*) tr_h[4:0] = 10001(Hspice) (*b*) Correlations between tr_h[4:0] and EQ

## 4 Simulation Results

### 4.1 Simulation in Normal Transmission State

Figure 8 illustrates output waveforms and eye diagram in normal transmission state, we set tr[4:0] = 11011, common mode voltage is 1.2 V, EQ is 6 dB, and the output serial data baud rate is 6.25 Gbps.

Table 2 lists the simulation result in different corner. Take TT as a example, the output differential swing is 979.35 mV, EQ is 6.08 dB, the rise and fall time is

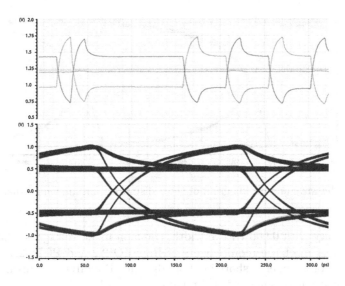

**Fig. 8.** The output waveform and eye diagram of transmitter

**Table 2.** The simulation result in normal transmission state

| Index | RapidIO$^\alpha$ | RapidIO$^\beta$ | PCIE2.1 | TT | SS | FF |
|---|---|---|---|---|---|---|
| VTX-DIFF-PP | 0.4–0.75 V | 0.8–1.2 V | 0.8–1.2 V | 0.98 V | 0.90 V | 1.0 V |
| VTX-DE-RATIO | * | * | 5.5–6.5 dB | 6.08 dB | 5.62 dB | 6.47 dB |
| T_tr,T_tf | >30 ps | >30 ps | >0.15 UI | 68 ps | 74 ps | 63.7 ps |
| T_Vcm | 0.1–1.7 V | 0.1–1.7 V | 0–3.6 V | 1.234 V | 1.05248 V | 1.4074 V |
|  | 0.63–1.1 V | 0.63–1.1 V |  |  |  |  |
| TTXEYE | >0.7 UI | >0.7 UI | >=0.75 UI | 0.906 UI | 0.905 UI | 0.906 UI |

$\alpha$ represents the RapidIO2.2 Level 2 (short distance);
$\beta$ represents the RapidIO2.2 Level 2 (long distance);
$VTXDIFFPP$: The differential output peak voltage;
$VTXDERATIO$: The pre-emphasis gain;
$T\_tr$: The rise time of eye diagram;
$T\_tf$: The fall time of eye diagram;
$T - Vcm$: The common mode voltage;
$TTX - EYE$: The width of eye diagram.

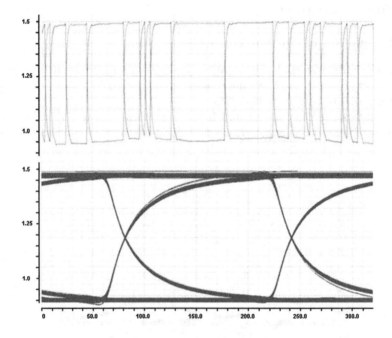

**Fig. 9.** The wave and eye diagram of short-distance transmission (corner: TT)

68ps on average with 0.906-UI eye width, common mode voltage is 1.234 V. All the parameters meet the requirements of RapidIO 2.2 and PCIE 2.1. Because of the length of channel is short in short distance RapidIO2.2, pre-emphasis is unnecessary and need some extra simulation.

For the situation of short-distance transmission, The attenuation can be ignored due to the channel is short, so we set the control bits tr[4:0] = 0000 to close pre-emphasis and lower the signal swing to decrease power consumption. Figure 9 shows the simulation wave when the level[5:0] = 100011, the output wave swing is 0.55 V in this moment.

### 4.2 Simulation with Package

Figure 10 shows the simulation result when the pre-emphasis is 6 dB, common mode level is 1.2 V and the input data is PRBS7 code. The output signal differential swing of driver is about 1 V, and waveform becomes smooth through the channel due to the pre-emphasis offsets the decay of high frequency. The swing is reduced to approximately 0.6 V which is approximately equivalent to 10 dB attenuation.

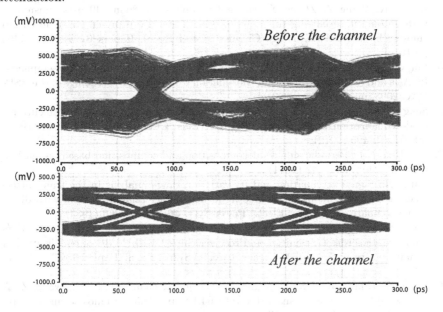

**Fig. 10.** The overall structure of transmitter

## 5    Conclusion

This paper proposes a transmitter based on 40 nm process, which can work at 2.5–6.25 GB/s data rate, offer 0–6 dB programmable pre-emphasis, common mode, and meeting PCIE2.1 and RapidIO2.2 protocols. By using simple DAC and amplifier, this design not only realizes traditional function of driver circuit, but also adds extensibility as well as programmable ability with little complexity which is the trend in multi-protocol supporting circuit design. The most difficult part of this design is that it needs more transistors due to the large total current of branches.

**Acknowledgment.** This paper is supported by the research of shared memory architecture for a general purpose microprocessor (No. 61472432).

# References

1. Balamurugan, G., Kennedy, J., Banerjee, G., Jaussi, J.E., Mansuri, M., O'Mahony, F., Casper, B., Mooney, R.: A scalable 5c15 Gbps, 14c75 mw low-power i/o transceiver in 65 nm cmos. IEEE J. Solid-State Circuits **43**(4), 1010–1019 (2008)
2. Bassi, M., Radice, F., Bruccoleri, M., Erba, S., Mazzanti, A.: A high-swing 45 gb/s hybrid voltage and current-mode pam-4 transmitter in 28 nm cmos fdsoi. IEEE J. Solid-State Circuits **51**(11), 2702–2715 (2016)
3. Hu, C., Chen, S., Huang, P., Liu, Y., Chen, J.: Evaluating the single event sensitivity of dynamic comparator in 5 Gbps serdes. Ieice Electron. Express **12**(23), 1–10 (2015)
4. Huang, K., Wang, Z., Zheng, X., Zhang, C., Wang, Z.: A 80 mw 40 gb/s transmitter with automatic serializing time window search and 2-tap pre-emphasis in 65 nm cmos technology. IEEE Trans. Circuits Syst. I Regul. Papers **62**(5), 1441–1450 (2015)
5. Lin, C.H., Wang, C.H., Jou, S.J.: 5 Gbps serial link transmitter with pre-emphasis. In: Asia and South Pacific Design Automation Conference, Proceedings of the ASP-DAC 2003, pp. 795–800 (2003)
6. Song, Y.H., Palermo, S.: A 6-Gbit/s hybrid voltage-mode transmitter with current-mode equalization in 90-nm cmos. IEEE Trans. Circuits Syst. II Express Briefs **59**(8), 491–495 (2012)
7. Yan-Hua, X.I.: Periodic signal's decomposition and composition based on matlab. Comput. Mod. 234–242 (2011)
8. Yang, N.: Signal attenuation and its variation range analysis in the transmitter-receiver input circuit of the double frequency carrier relaying system with directional comparison. Autom. Electr. Power Syst. **46**(2), 362–366 (1983)
9. Yuan, S., Wu, L., Wang, Z., Zheng, X., Zhang, C., Wang, Z.: A 70 mw 25 GB/s quarter-rate serdes transmitter and receiver chipset with 40 dB of equalization in 65 nm cmos technology. IEEE Trans. Circuits Syst. I Regul. Papers **63**(7), 939–949 (2016)
10. Zhou, N., Huang, K., Lve, F., Wang, Z., Zheng, X., Zhang, C., Li, F., Wang, Z.: A 76 mw 40-GB/s serdes transmitter with 64:1 mux in 65-nm cmos technology. In: International Conference on Electronics Information and Emergency Communication, pp. 155–158 (2016)
11. Zite, S.E.: Design of a unit current cell for a 12-bit 3.2 GHz current steering digital-to-analog converter (2006)

# A Radiation-Immune Low-Jitter High-Frequency PLL for SerDes

Hengzhou Yuan, Jianjun Chen, Bin Liang, and Yang Guo[✉]

College of Computer, National University of Defense Technology,
Deya Str. 109, Changsha 410073, People's Republic of China
guoyang@nudt.edu.cn

**Abstract.** A radiation-tolerant phase-locked loop (PLL) is designed in 65 nm CMOS technology. A double feedback loop self-sampling structure is proposed to improve the anti-radiation capability. A High matched current-based charge pump is hardened by using sensitive nodes compression and transformation technology. The simulation results show that the proposed PLL has no significant variations under heavy-ion and it could output good jitter signals with high frequency.

**Keywords:** PLL · Radiation-Harden · Low-Noise · High frequency
Double loop · Self-Sampling

## 1 Introduction

The performance of aerospace chip is improving rapidly. To meet the demand of high data rates transmission, SerDes (SERializer-DESerializer) is widely used. Increasing the communication data rates lead a more stringent specification the PLL clock jitter in terms of both random Gaussian jitter and deterministic jitter [1].

Previous studies have demonstrated that PLLs are vulnerable to single-event transients (SETs), resulting in missing pulses and phase displacement [2]. Due to single-event effects (SEEs), high energy particle will pass through semiconductor materials and deposit charge in sensitive devices. It is challenging to design high-performance phase-locked loops (PLLs) for space applications.

The traditional harden technology is unsuitable for PLL in SerDes. Because the existing technology in radiation-hardened PLL is based on the trade-off between anti-radiation ability and performance(jitter and frequency). The charge pump (CP) was identified as the most sensitive module. A voltage-based charge pump was proposed to significantly improve the single-event tolerance with considerable noise degradation [3]. Besides, the voltage-controlled oscillator (VCO) was studied to present increased susceptibility to single-event upsets (SEUs) in advanced technology nodes [4]. Triple modular redundancy (TMR) technique has been commonly utilized in the VCO circuit and frequency divider [5] to eliminate soft errors, but with great area and frequency penalties

In this paper, a radiation-immune PLL is proposed to improve the anti-radiation ability without degradation of jitter and frequency performance. In Sect. 2, PLL radiation hardening by process in 65 nm process is discussed. In Sect. 3, the novel

© Springer Nature Singapore Pte Ltd. 2018
W. Xu et al. (Eds.): NCCET 2017, CCIS 600, pp. 45–51, 2018.
https://doi.org/10.1007/978-981-10-7844-6_5

double loop feedback self-sampling structure is proposed to remove the SET effect of divider and PFD. Current-based charge pump with sensitivity node transformation technology is proposed to improve the jitter performance of PLL. In Sect. 4, layout design and simulation analysis are discussed. In Sect. 5, conclusion is given.

## 2 Radiation Hardening by Process

The 65 nm process provides deep Nwell technology to achieve low noise. From the aspect of radiation-hardening, the deep Nwell can also absorb the SET current of heavy-ion strike.

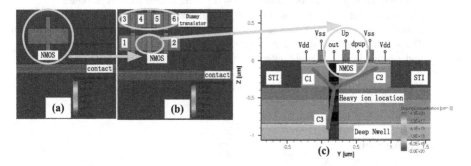

**Fig. 1.** Layout harden with dummy transistors by deep Nwell technology

The heavy-ion simulations have been performed using TCAD software. The simulation result is shown in Fig. 1. LET is 37.6 meV·cm2/mg, and the ion strike is irradiated normal to the chip surface.

As shown in Fig. 2(a), the SET current is all absorbed by the deep Nwell and the dummy transistor. The Fig. 2(b) shows that the voltage has no significant variations under heavy-ion when switch gate and the dummy transistors are built in deep Nwell.

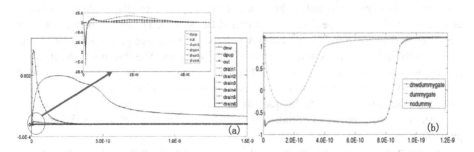

**Fig. 2.** SET current and voltage variation

## 3 Radiation Hardening by Design

Traditional PLL is single loop negative feedback system consists of PFD, CP, LPF, DIV and VCO. When SET happen at one of the five components, it may lead the PLL out of lock state and the error bit rate of SerDes will increase.

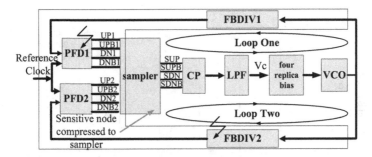

**Fig. 3.** SET current and voltage variation Double feedback loop self-sampling PLL

The PFD and Divider are digital circuits and are very sensitive to SET, because they use the minimum gate length. To improve the anti-SET capability, we adapt the double loop to feedback the divided signals from VCO to PFD in Fig. 3. The advantage of this structure is that, it will largely reduce the sensitivity of feedback loops. As shown in Fig. 4, if the iron strikes the PFD1 and FBDIV2, it will only induce one loop to produce error signal in UP1 or UP2. The other loop operation remains good and will produce right UP and DN signals at the same time. The sampling circuit in Fig. 4 will let correct up and down signals(SUP, SUPB, SDN, SDNB) pass through. This double loop structure will compress the sensitive nodes of all the FBDIV and PFD into AND gates in sampler.

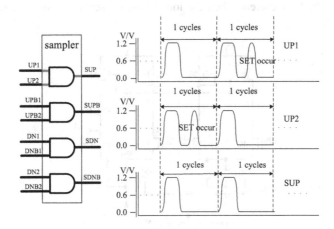

**Fig. 4.** Function of sampler

Previous study of voltage-based CP (V-CP) [4] employs large reference spurs and phase noise, which is not suitable for SerDes application. The proposed CP is especially suitable for low jitter application because its mismatch is quite low, as shown in Fig. 5. The differential structure of CP we used in this paper has alleviated the charge sharing of traditional charge pump by using two pairs of charge pump. It is similar to the structure of [6].

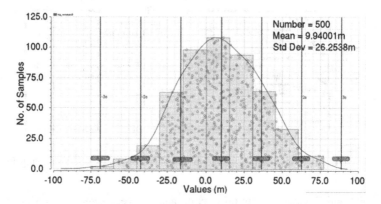

**Fig. 5.** The Current Waveform and DC mismatch

To improve the anti-radiation ability of CP, M8 is added. It is called sensitive nodes transformation technology, as shown in Fig. 6, the sensitive nodes of replica charge pump in the left is compressed to M8. As the sensitive nodes of CP are compressed into M8, the switch gate should be hardened at circuit level and layout level. As shown in Fig. 6, the original switch gate is one NMOS transistor, to absorb the large SET current, the dummy transistors are located round the switch gate. The gates of dummy transistors are all connected to ground and the drains of dummy transistors are all connected to power rail. The dummy transistors will not affect the operation of CP, but it will absorb the SET current when the ion strikes the sensitive nodes of CP.

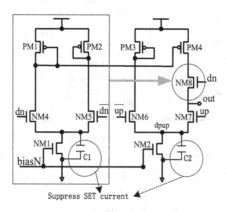

**Fig. 6.** Circuits of charge pump

## 4   Layout Design and Simulation Analysis

The test chip layout of PLL is shown in Fig. 7. We simulate the PLL with 65 nm process model to testify the low jitter and high frequency performance of this PLL. The RMS jitter and stability are calculated by Matlab program. The result is shown in Fig. 8. The Rj will not exceed 2.17 ps and the Dj is 6.5 ps, when the PLL is locked at 3.125 GHz.

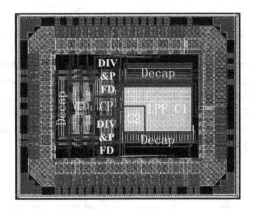

**Fig. 7.**  Test chip layout of PLL

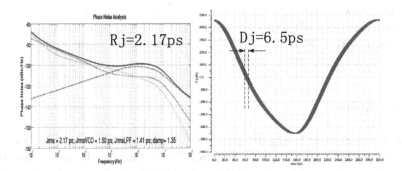

**Fig. 8.**  PLL output noise

The SET current model is added when the PLL is locked at 3.125 GHz, the unit interval of SerDes is 320 ps. To sample the correct RX data, the clock skew can not exceed 0.5UI. As shown in Fig. 9, the maximum skew that the VCO would produce is 41.64 ps, and the recovery time is 67 ns. Theoretically, the SET would not happen again in the 67 ns. The SerDes system will not have error data when SET happened in PLL.

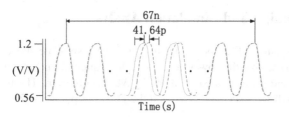

**Fig. 9.** SET current and voltage variation

We compare the proposed PLL with some recently published papers in Table 1. The deterministic jitter is 6.5 ps@65 nm. The integrated RMS jitter is 2.17 ps@65 nm. The jitter performance is good among all the references means that the charge pump can achieve better jitter performance than other PLLs. The proposed PLL will not decrease the error data rate when the PLL has SEE effects. Although Ref. [7] is more advanced in jitter and power consumption, but it is not suitable for radiation hardening because of interpolative phase-coupled oscillator DCO structure, the SET effect will lead the PLL out of lock state.

**Table 1.** Comparison among Different PLLs

| Ref. Year | [7] 2014 | [8] 2010 | [9] 2016 | This Work |
| --- | --- | --- | --- | --- |
| Tech.(nm) | 65 | 45 | 130 | 65 |
| Power(V) | 0.8 | 2.5 | 1.2 | 1.2 |
| Power (mW) | 0.78 | 70 | 8.54 | 43.6 |
| RMS Jitter(ps) | 1.7@0.9 GHz | 0.99@2.5 GHz | 7.1@0.5 GHz | 2.17@3.125 GHz |
| Output [MHz] | 390–1410 | 2500 | 500 | 1250–3125 |
| Input [MHz] | 40–350 | 100 | 100 | 100–300 |

## 5    Conclusion

A radiation-tolerant PLL was designed and fabricated in 65 nm process. The PLL hardened by process was discussed. Various radiation hardening by design techniques were employed in order to have comprehensive radiation tolerance. A novel double loop feedback self-sampling structure was proposed to mitigate radiation effects of divider and PFD. Radiation hardened current based CP with sensitive nodes transformation technology was proposed to make the CP have smaller sensitive nodes. The simulation results demonstrate the good jitter performance of PLL when SET happens.

**Acknowledgments.** This research was supported by National Natural Science Foundation of China Program (No. 61504169).

# References

1. Wadekar, J., et al.: A 0.5–4 GHz programmable-bandwidth fractional-N PLL for multi-protocol SERDES in 28 nm CMOS. In: 2016 29th International Conference on VLSI Design, vol. 41, pp. 236–239 (2016)
2. Kauppila, A.V., et al.: Analysis of the single event effects for a 90 nm CMOS phase-locked loop. In: Proceedings of the Radiation Effects Components and Systems (RADECS), pp. 201–206, September 2009
3. Loveless, T.D., et al.: A hardened-by-design technique for RF digital phase-locked loops. IEEE Trans. Nucl. Sci. **53**(6), 3432–3438 (2006)
4. Loveless, T.D., et al.: A single-event-hardened phase-locked loop fabricated in 130 nm CMOS. IEEE Trans. Nucl. Sci. **54**(6), 2012–2020 (2007)
5. She, X., et al.: Single event transient tolerant frequency divider. IET Comput. Digit. Tech. **8**(3), 140–147 (2014)
6. Yuan, H., et al.: A low-jitter self-biased phase-locked loop for SerDes. In: ISOCC 2016, pp. 550–554 (2016)
7. Deng, W., et al.: A 0.0066 mm 2780 µW fully synthesizable PLL with a current-output DAC and an interpolative phase-coupled oscillator using edge-injection technique. In: ISSCC Digest of Technical Papers, pp. 266–267, February 2014
8. Fischette, D., et al.: A 45 nm SOI-CMOS dual-PLL processor clock system for multi-protocol I/O. In: ISSCC Digest of Technical Papers, pp. 246–247, February 2010
9. Brownlee, M., et al.: Single-event transient characterization of a radiation-tolerant charge-pump phase-locked loop fabricated in 130 nm PD-SOI technology. IEEE Trans. Nucl. Sci. **63**(4), 2402–2408 (2016)

# A High Throughput Power-Efficient Optical Memory Subsystem for Kilo-Core Processor

Quanyou Feng[✉], Chao Peng, Shuangyin Ren, Hongwei Zhou,
and Rangyu Deng

National University of Defense Technology, Changsha 410073, China
fengquanyou@nudt.edu.cn

**Abstract.** High throughput and power-efficient processor-memory communications are of great importance for kilo-core processor design. This paper proposes a hybrid photonic architecture for such communications. Bandwidth-efficient photonic burst switching is used for memory accesses between last-level HBM caches and off-chip HMC memory pools. Simulation results show that the hybrid network achieves up to 25% of system speedup and up to 10 times of energy savings, when compared to conventional electric interconnects.

**Keywords:** Photonic interconnects · HBM · Memory subsystem

## 1 Introduction

For the coming Exascale computing era [1], manycore processors play an essential role in achieving such performance goals. Recent years, manycore processors have already been demonstrated by integrating more and more computing cores on a single die. For example, the Tilera TILE-Gx100-cores processor [2] and phytium's 64-core chip named "Mars" [3]. With the trend of manycore chips towards increasing number of cores, for example, 1000 cores [4], memory subsystem design, which must sustain the enormous demand for off-chip memory accesses in an energy-efficient manner, has become a critical challenge.

Processor-memory interconnects have special constraints when manycore processor scales up. It has been discovered that projected scaling of electrical processor-memory network appears unlikely to meet the enormous demand for off-chip bandwidth while satisfying stringent power budget [5]. In this work, we propose a hybrid optical memory subsystem for kilo-core processor chips, which leverages the recent advent of new memory technologies, namely the high-bandwidth memory (HBM) [6] and hybrid memory cube (HMC) [7]. The hybrid system utilizes high-bandwidth HBMs as the on-chip last-level caches and high-speed off-chip HMCs as memory pools; photonic burst switching (PBS) is used for processor-memory transmission. PBS is an adaptation of optical burst switching [8] for chip-scale network using silicon photonic devices. The PBS network meets the enormous bandwidth demand and stringent energy constraints by using high-speed low-power CMOS-compatible photonic devices. Furthermore,it has higher bandwidth utilization than wavelength routing and optical circuit-switching because of sub-wavelength optical switching.

© Springer Nature Singapore Pte Ltd. 2018
W. Xu et al. (Eds.): NCCET 2017, CCIS 600, pp. 52–62, 2018.
https://doi.org/10.1007/978-981-10-7844-6_6

We examine the system feasibility and performances using physically-accurate interconnects simulation environment. Both synthetic traffic patterns and real workloads traces are used to evaluate the architecture. Simulation results show that the hybrid network achieves up to 25% of system speedup and up to 10 times of energy savings, compared to conventional electric interconnects.

The rest of this paper is organized as follows. Section 2 summarizes state of the art on photonic chip-scale networks and presents related backgrounds on emerging memory technologies. Section 3 details the hybrid memory subsystem architecture. Section 4 presents the simulation results and discussions. Conclusions and future work are included in Sect. 5.

## 2 Related Works

### 2.1 Photonic Chip-Scale Network

CMOS-compatible photonic devices, including modulators, detector, waveguides and optical switches have all been demonstrated by silicon photonic technology [9] and they have paved the way for optical chip-scale network design. For example, Vantrease et al. [10] used a dense wavelength division multiplexed crossbar to connect off-stack memory modules; Hendry et al. [11] proposed an optical circuit-switched memory access scheme. In these systems, photonic devices, memory devices and logic circuits are stacked together by three dimensional integration (3D-I) [12].

Figure 1 illustrates two basic switching elements for constructing complex optical switches [13]. As the electrical parameters of micro-ring resonators' are adjusted, the photonic path in waveguides can be switched on or off, thus optical messages can go straight through or turn around.

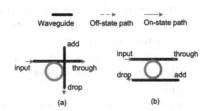

**Fig. 1.** $1 \times 2$ optical switches. (a) Crossing. (b) Parallel.

### 2.2 HMCs and HBMs

In a single HMC package [7], multiple memory dies and one logic die are stacked together, using through-silicon via (TSV) technology and micro-bumps (see Fig. 2). Memory is organized into vaults. Each vault is functionally and operationally independent. HMC uses standard DRAM cells but it has more data banks than classic DRAM memory of the same size. The HMC interface uses serial IOs, which is incompatible with current DDRn buses.

HBM stacks up multiple DRAM devices across a number of independent interfaces called channels, which is optimized for high-bandwidth operations. As shown in Fig. 3, each channel provides access to an independent set of DRAM banks. Each memory controller is independently timed and controlled. The HBM memory uses wider parallel bus than current DDRn memories and offers lower latency when directly attached to user chip die within the same package [6].

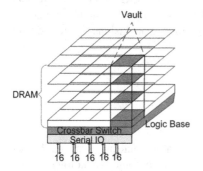

**Fig. 2.** HMC architecture

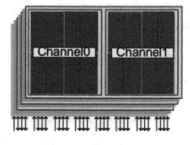

8 channels, 128bansks, ~1600pins

**Fig. 3.** HBM architecture.

HBM and HMC both provide high-bandwidth memory operations by means of multiple independent access channels. However, a HMC would work as a separate memory chip while a HBM must be integrated into the user chip package.

## 3   The Optical Memory Subsystem Architecture

Scientific applications usually require significant computing power in the form of high bandwidth data access and streaming processing capabilities within a low power budget. Access of continuous memory blocks using DMA occurs frequently. Main memory bandwidth, without doubt, has become the key bottleneck in many-core systems. Recent advances in silicon photonics and memory technologies have brought new opportunities for such challenges.

Figure 4 illustrates our proposed optical memory subsystem for kilo-core processors. Directly attached HBMs are used as on-chip last-level caches (LLCs) which provides high-bandwidth low-latency memory access by utilizing the wide parallel buses; Off-chip memory pools built on HMCs deliver an order of magnitude more bandwidth than current DDRx solutions. LLCs and memory pools are interconnected by a photonic interconnection network. On-chip edge node of the optical network aggregates traffics for LLCs while off-chip edge node provides access to memory pools. Optical messages are transmitted and routed by photonic cross-connects in the core node. In the system, photonic IOs and switches are stacked with the electronic processor plane using 3DI. On the interconnect plane, optical router nodes and memory access interface nodes are usually arranged in a simple mesh for ease of chip layout and integration.

In this following section, we first examine the chip-scale photonic interconnects architecture, which is a burst-switched optical mesh, and then we describe HBM LLCs and HMC memory pools.

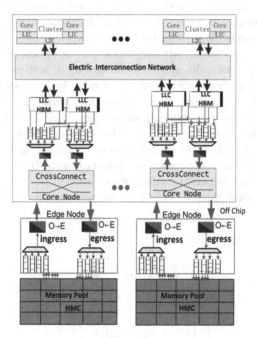

**Fig. 4.** Chip-scale optical burst-switching interconnects for memory subsystem of kilo-core processor.

## 3.1 The Burst-Switched Photonic Mesh

Generally, photonic links have a significant static energy cost in thermal tuning circuits and optical laser sources, which can be much higher than the static energy cost of electrical links [9]. Hence, networks designed using photonic links need to have high utilization to offset the large static energy overhead. Existing photonic chip-scale network schemes, including wavelength routing and optical circuit-switching [11], suffer from poor bandwidth utilization since an exclusive wavelength channel must be reserved from source to destination for the whole duration of packet transmission. The large portion of static energy overhead in these networks actually degrades their energy efficiency.

Our proposed optical mesh uses a different switching protocol, namely photonic burst switching, in which no exclusive wavelength channel has to be reserved from source to destination for the whole duration of packet transmission. Packets (including memory read/write requests, memory response) from LLC nodes are buffered at the ingress nodes and aggregated into bursts. These bursts are optically switched by the core nodes and disassembled at the egress node in order to be relayed to the destination (see Fig. 4).

Our model uses a Just-Enough-Time (JET) signaling scheme [8]. A burst control header packet (BCP) is created and sent by the ingress node an offset time before the burst is sent. It contains information including the burst arrival time, burst size, destination. This BCP packet is electronically processed at every core node. With the control information carried within BCP packets, optical core nodes reserves the appropriate forwarding path for the optical bursts from ingress to egress. The wavelength channel on a link used by the burst will be released as soon as the burst passes through. Switching optical bursts achieves, to certain extent, a balance between switching coarse-grained optical circuits and switching fine-grained optical packets/cells, and combines the best of both paradigms [11].

Figure 5 shows the internal structure of a core node. In the optical mesh, core nodes are responsible for processing BCPs while the bursts are switched without electro-optical conversion from ingress point to egress node. Core node is built on top of a dynamically configurable cross connect. Optical cross connects can be constructed with cascaded switching element based on micro-ring resonator devices [13]. The cross connects in core node follow the commands of control units. The control unit makes its decisions by first processing control information carried in BCPs and then reserves the output ports, wavelength channels before the optical bursts arrive.

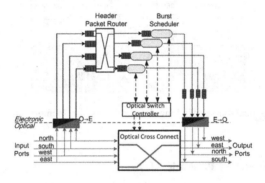

**Fig. 5.** A general architecture of OBS router

Edge node around the chip periphery relays on-chip memory requests to off-chip memory pools and vice versa. Off-chip photonic IO signaling is achieved through lateral coupling by through inverse-taper optical mode converters [14]. In this edge node, optical bursts of read requests are first disassembled and then transmitted to corresponding HMC channels; data responses are aggregated into optical bursts and sent back to LLCs. Write requests with data are first disassembled and then directly sent to destination HMCs.

## 3.2  Last-Level HBM Cache

Three main observations inspire us that HBMs fit well when used as last-level caches.

First, the HBM devices are optimized for high-bandwidth operation to a stack of multiple DRAM devices across a number of independent channels. It is anticipated that each DRAM stack will support up to 8 channels [6]. Each channel provides access to an independent set of DRAM banks. Requests from one channel may not access data attached to a different channel. Channels are independently clocked, and need not be synchronous. Besides, the HBM memory uses wider parallel bus than current DDRn memories. Wider buses and multiple independent channels offer a large amount of parallelism for cache accesses.

Second, HBM memory is generally directly attached to processor chip die within the same package, thus it offers lower latency than off-chip accesses.

Third, HBMs have larger capacity than traditional on-chip caches, it may work as a large memory page buffer for off-chip main memory and miss rates may be very low if aggressive prefetching schemes are adopted.

### 3.3   External HMC Memory Pool

Kilo-core processing is bringing incredible advances to supercomputing and advanced networking systems—advances that require a new level of memory efficiency and performance. Hybrid memory cubes (HMCs) are projected to maximize the full potential of these high-performance systems [7]. The Hybrid Memory Cube (HMC) is an emerging main memory technology that leverages advances in 3D fabrication techniques to create a memory device with several DRAM dies stacked on top of a CMOS logic layer. The logic layer at the base of each stack contains several DRAM memory controllers that communicate with the host over high speed serial links using an abstracted packet interface. Each memory controller is connected to several memory banks in the DRAM stack with Through-Silicon Vias (TSVs). The TSV connections combined with the presence of multiple memory controllers near the memory arrays form a device that exposes significant memory-level parallelism and is capable of delivering an order of magnitude more bandwidth than current DDRx solutions.

System designers have the option of using the HMC in a scalable module form factor as "memory pool" for optimized power efficiency. As Fig. 6 shows, in addition to being directly attached to a processor socket as a single device, the HMCs can be chained together to form a diverse set of topologies with unique performance

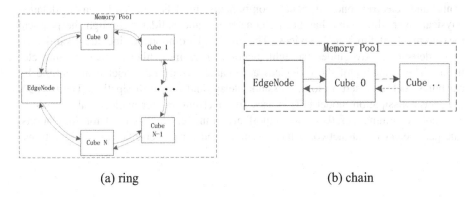

(a) ring                                        (b) chain

**Fig. 6.** Topologies for the memory pool (a) ring (b) chain.

characteristics, for example rings and linear chains. In theory any number of cubes can be connected together to extend the capacity of the memory system. However, practical limits on the number of cubes and types of topologies that can be implemented do exist. A network of up to 8 cubes has been studied [7].

It has been found that today's CPU protocols such as coherent caches pose a problem for high-throughput HMC memory systems [15]. That is the other reason we use HMCs only as off-chip memory pools since there are only reads and writes between LLCs and memory pools, no coherent requests are involved.

## 4   Simulation and Results

To evaluate the performance of aforementioned hybrid photonic memory subsystem (HPMS, see Fig. 4), we compare it with a baseline 2D concentrated mesh electric network (CMesh). In both architectures, a 256-core processor is considered; 16 cores with private L1 cache and a shared L2 cache constitute a cluster; HBMs are used as LLCs; HMCs are used as off-chip memory pools. Clusters and LLCs are connected by on-chip electric meshes. The only difference is that a LLC in CMesh is directly connected to an exclusive off-chip HMC memory pool using electrical serial IOs while LLCs in HPMS are connected to off-chip HMCs using photonic burst-switched interconnects.

Two sets of benchmarks, both standard synthetic traces and real application traces are studied. Synthetic benchmarks help to identify system metrics, such as traffic patterns and energy savings; application traces focus on system speedups, e.g. interconnect delays.

### 4.1   Simulation Setups

Our study uses the PhoenixSim simulator [16] which is a physical-level accurate simulation platform for optical network research. The HBM LLCs modules, HMC memory pool modules and an optical burst switching module are developed and integrated into the platform.

The simulator allows us to capture physical-layer details of both optical components and electric ones. Optical components models are built on a detailed physical-layer library that has been characterized and validated through the physical measurement of fabricated devices. The modeled components include modulators, photo-detectors, waveguides (straight, bending, crossing), filters, and switching elements. The behavior of these devices are characterized and modeled at runtime by attributes such as insertion loss, crosstalk, delay, and power dissipation. The ORION 2.0 power dissipation model [17] is used for electronic router in electrical meshes.

Table 1 summarizes the more important parameters that is used for simulations. The parameters for all networks have been chosen for power-efficient configurations.

**Table 1.** Table captions should be placed above the tables.

| Parameter | CMesh | HPMS |
|---|---|---|
| *Cluster Configuration* | | |
| Core &E-mesh Freq. | 2 GHz | 2 GHz |
| L1C capacity | 32 K | 32 K |
| L2C capacity | 2 M | 2 M |
| *HBM LLC* | | |
| Number of Channels | 2 | 2 |
| Channel density | 2 GB | 2 GB |
| Page Size | 2 KB | 2 KB |
| *HMC memory pool* | | |
| # of Cubes per pool | 2 | 2 |
| # of Links per cube | 8 | 8 |
| Serial IO | 10 GBps | 10 GBps |
| Cube bandwidth | 320 GBps | 320 GBps |
| *Photonic Interconnects* | | |
| Data rate (per wavelength) | NA | 10 GBps |
| # of wavelength | NA | 16 |
| Topology of optical interconnects | NA | 2 × 2 Mesh |
| Resonator witching time | NA | 30 ps |
| Dynamic energy of a switch element | NA | 375 fJ |
| Static energy of a switch element | NA | 400 μJps |
| Detector energy | NA | 50 fJ/bit |

## 4.2   Results for Synthetic Traffic Patterns

The synthetic traces used in the simulations include the uniform and the hotspot. In the uniform traffic pattern, each L2Cs sends memory requests to all LLCs with the same probability. In the hotspot traffic pattern, one LLC is designated as hotspot, which receives requests from all L2Cs in addition to the regular uniform traffic.

Here, we focus on power savings because processor-memory network generally has stringent power budget. Figure 7 shows the metric of energy efficiency: performance gained for every unit of energy spent, which is effectively a measure of a network's efficiency. As shown in Fig. 7, the traffics with small messages (64 Bytes per cache-line) perform poorly on photonic processor-memory networks. The reason is that the large amount of static energy overhead of photonic devices cannot be compensated by small-size message transmission. So, we enlarge the message size (256 Bytes per cache-line) and simulate again. As a result, the photonic network, HPMS, achieves the most noticeable improvements in energy efficiency (more than 10 times) for uniform random traffic.

The reason for this is twofold. First, large bulk data movement potentially offsets the static power overhead of photonic links discussed in Sect. 3.1, so the photonic memory access scheme, HPMS, shows higher energy efficiency than the electric CMesh.

Second, photonic HPMS utilizes one-way signaling scheme and sub-wavelength switching, which means no wavelength channel has to be reserved exclusively from source to destination for the whole duration of packet transmission, resulting in improved bandwidth utilization and considerable reduction of blocking probability on photonic links.

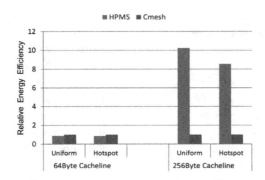

**Fig. 7.** Simulation results of relative energy efficiency gains for proposed architecture.

### 4.3 Results for Real Workload Traces

Two application traces are considered: Radix integer sorting (Radix) and Barnes. The Barnes application implements the Barnes-Hut method to simulate the interaction of a system of bodies (N-body problem). Barnes and Radix come from the SPLASH-2 sets. These applications represent typical features of scientific applications. The Graphite simulator [18] is used to collect their traces, which provides accurate modeling for the memory subsystems (including cache hierarchies with full cache coherence) and cores. Important parameters (L1 cache/LLC cache, coherence scheme) are selected to mimic real execution environment. The default dataset is scaled up appropriately to ensure that statistical values of normalized metrics converge to a stable state after long simulation duration. L2C traces of Graphite are fed into aforementioned simulation modules, since our simulation focuses on the communications between LLCs and memory pools only.

Figure 8 shows the results of average transaction latency for the two traces. Particularly, HPMS shows a moderate amount of latency reduction, i.e., 17.5% ~ 25.9% against CMesh. We find that these performance gains mainly come from the smooth pass-through of optical links for off-chip access in photonic HPMS, while the overhead of electric serial IOs in Cmesh consumes a large amount of transaction delays.

Generally speaking, our simulation methodology suffers from some drawbacks. A unified environment (including compiler chain, system call support, cache coherence operations) for full system simulation is missing. Only memory traces are extracted. Many aspects of kilo-core system runtime have been abstracted away at a higher level. Nevertheless, using the physically-accurate network-level simulation environment, the results still highlight the advantages of our hybrid architecture over conventional electrical schemes in terms of energy savings and system scalability.

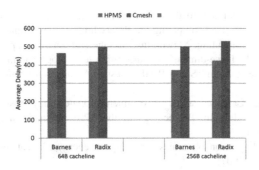

**Fig. 8.** Simulation results of average delay for barnes and radix.

# 5 Conclusions and Future Work

This paper proposes a hybrid photonic burst-switched architecture for processor-memory communications. It uses bandwidth-efficient photonic burst switching for memory access between HBM last-level caches and off-chip HMC memory pools. Simulations results using synthetic and real workload traces show that the hybrid network achieves considerable improvements in terms of network latency and power consumption, when compared to conventional electrical mesh network. Other aspects, e.g. cache hierarchies and optimal scheduling for optical bursts are under study.

**Acknowledgement.** This research is supported by the grants from National Natural Science Foundation of China (Grant No. 61402502). Also, NSF 61402497 and 61472432 of China support our research.

# References

1. Agerwala, T.: Exascale computing: the challenges and opportunities in the next decade. In: 16th Proceedings of the IEEE Symposium on HPCA, p. 1 (2010)
2. TILEGx Homepage. http://www.tilera.com/products/TILE-Gx.php. Accessed 29 Dec 2011
3. Zhang, C.: Mars: a 64-core ARMv8 processor. In: 27th Hot Chips (2015)
4. Borkar, S.: Thousand core chips: a technology perspective. In: Proceedings of the 44th ACM/IEEE Design Automation Conference, pp. 746–749 (2007)
5. Sanchez, D., et al.: An analysis of on-chip interconnection networks for large-scale chip multiprocessors. ACM Trans. Archit. Code Optim. **7**(1), 4 (2010)
6. JEDEC Homepage. https://www.jedec.org/. Accessed 21 June 2017
7. HMC Homepage. http://www.hybridmemorycude.org/. Accessed 21 June 2017
8. Qiao, C.M., Yoo, M.S.: Optical burst switching (OBS) - a new paradigm for an optical internet. J. High Speed Netw. **8**(1), 69–84 (1999)
9. Shacham, A., Bergman, K., Carloni, L.P.: Photonic networks-on-chip for future generations of chip multiprocessors. IEEE Trans. Comput. **57**(9), 1246–1260 (2008)
10. Vantrease, D., et al.: Corona: system implications of emerging nanophotonic technology. In: Proceedings of the 35th International Symposium on Computer Architecture, pp. 153–164 (2008)

11. Hendry, G., et al.: Circuit-switched memory access in photonic interconnection networks for high-performance embedded computing. In: Proceedings of the International Conference for High Performance Computing, Networking, Storage and Analysis, pp. 1–12 (2010)
12. Koyanagi, M., et al.: Three-dimensional integration technology and integrated systems. In: Proceedings of the Asia and South Pacific Design Automation Conference, pp. 409–415 (2009)
13. Poon, A.W., et al.: Cascaded active silicon microresonator array cross-connect circuits for WDM networks-on-chip. In: Proceedings of the SPIE International Society for Optical Engineering (2008)
14. Barwicz, T., et al.: Silicon photonics for compact, energy-efficient interconnects. J. Opt. Netw. **6**(1), 63–73 (2007)
15. Rosenfeld, P.: Performance evaluation of the hybrid memory cube. Dissertation of the University of Maryland (2014)
16. Chan, J., et al.: Phoenixsim: a simulator for physical-layer analysis of chip-scale photonic interconnection networks. In: Proceedings on Design, Automation and Test in Europe (2010)
17. Kahng, A.B., et al.: Orion 2.0: a fast and accurate NoC power and area model for early-stage design space exploration. In: Proceedings on Design, Automation and Test in Europe (2009)
18. Miller, J.E., et al.: Graphite: a distributed parallel simulator for multicores. In: 16th IEEE Symposium on High-Performance Computer Architecture, January 2010

# RBPCCM: Relax Blocking Parallel Collective Communication Mechanism Base on Hardware with Scalability

Xiu-jiang Ren[1], Zhou Zhou[1], Qing Peng[1], and Xiang-hui Xie[2(✉)]

[1] Jiangnan Institute of Computing Technology, Wuxi 214083, China
[2] State Key Laboratory of Mathematical Engineering and Advanced Computing,
Wuxi 214125, China
xie.xianghui@meac-skl.cn

**Abstract.** With the development of parallel computation, the scale of high performance computing system increases dramatically and the collective communication has become its bottleneck. The collective communication with the hardware support has the relatively high performance. However, scalability of collective communication is always a crucial problem, because the number of nodes involved is not fixed. This paper proposes the Relax Blocking Parallel Collective Communication Mechanism (RBPCCM) to improve the performance of the collective communication in parallel computation. This mechanism, cooperating hardware and software, implements the scalable collective communication by distributing collective resource allocation numbers. Furthermore, RBPCCM supports the implementation in various scales of endpoint, unconstrained by the interconnect network topology. A functional simulation model is built based on the system of Sunway Taihu Light to verify the correctness and scalability of this proposed method. The implementation of RBPCCM prototype is built based on the network interface, and a FPGA platform is constructed for performance test. It is testified that RBPCCM has the improvement as regards to delay performance from 2.4 to 37 times, compared with the Point-to-Point communication based on software.

**Keywords:** Collective communication · Scalable · Interconnection network

## 1 Introduction

High-performance computation systems usually adopt large-scale parallel processing structure, and they achieve powerful computation capability depending on the high-performance interconnect network including a large number of processors. Data-exchange and task-control among lots of processes are implemented by transferring messages in distributed parallel computations. The report "Some Challenges on Road from Petascale to Exascale" [1] released by IBM treats communication as one of five greatest challenges for future E level systems. It is reported that collective communications cost 60% computational time [2], and 80% communication resource in many large-scale science computational applications [3]. Nowadays, collective communications have been the bottleneck of high-performance computation, so its improvements have great significance.

© Springer Nature Singapore Pte Ltd. 2018
W. Xu et al. (Eds.): NCCET 2017, CCIS 600, pp. 63–75, 2018.
https://doi.org/10.1007/978-981-10-7844-6_7

This paper studies the collective communication in large-scale parallel computational systems and analyzes its implementation. A scalable Relax Blocking Parallel Collective Communication Mechanism (RBPCCM) is proposed. This mechanism accelerates collective communications and implements the parallel collective communication executions in different network structures and scales based on software-hardware cooperation. RBPCCM is implemented based on the network interface, and moreover its performance is tested in the FPGA verification system. Lastly, the feasibility and scalability of the proposed mechanism are verified in Sunway Taihu Light system. It is verified that RBPCCM improves the performance of collective communication 7–10 times averagely, and 30 times at the best case, comparing to the communication based on MPI point-to-point messages.

The remaining part of this paper is organized as: the related research, including the variety, implementation and development, about collective communication is analyzed in Sect. 2; RBPCCM mechanism is detailed descripted in Sect. 3; this proposed mechanism is verified in simulations and implemented based on the network interface; the performance of RBPCMM is evaluated on FPGA verification system and its results are analyzed thoroughly; this paper is summarized in Sect. 6.

## 2 Related Work

Modern high-performance computing system is built based on the large-scale parallel processing structure. It can accelerate the computation by running the program in parallel with several processing units. Large scale parallel programs are not simple combination of multiple serial programs. There are commonly a lot of synchronization, competition and interference among the objects which participate to the parallel executions. Therefore, cooperative control is required to make them accomplish a common task, and the collective communication is the most direct means to implement the global control mechanism. Some studies have shown that collective communication has become the bottleneck for high performance computers [2, 4]. How to improve the performance of collective communication is a subject worthy of further study.

### 2.1 Software Implementation

Since a large number of high-speed interconnection networks only support unicast communication, it is a common practice to use software algorithms to implement the collective communication between processes. These algorithms are mainly based on the LogP model [5] and its extended model. They improve the performance of collective communications by mining underlying features of network systems. The research in this field has been conducted widely [6, 7].

The software method can make full use of the computing power of the host processor, balance the communication calculation ratio and maximize system performance when dealing with the large amounts of data. However, the scheduling overhead of host processor is not enough to hide the communication delay when dealing with small amount of data, so it is difficult to improve the performance [4].

## 2.2  Hardware Implementation

Many studies have shown that hardware support is very helpful in improving performance. [8, 9] aimed to optimize collective operations for specific topologies. IBM's Blue Gene supercomputer included network-level hardware support for barrier and reduction operations. Furthermore, Blue Gene/P introduces a new message transmission architecture DCMF [10], which can provide support for the optimization of MPI aggregation communication algorithms [11]. In Blue Gene/Q, the collection communication is also optimized [12]. In the PERCS system [13], IBM uses customized hardware networks to speed up collective communications. [14] introduced NetAgg platform to improve the efficiency of network connections by using in-network middle box for collection operations. Cray's Aries network provides accelerated support for protocol operations alone.

Other studies have tried some full hardware approaches. Myrinet adds embedded processors to the network interface and loads different control program segments that can handle different collective communication [15]. Quadrics Elan network modified the loading mode for program [16], so these programs can locate the host's address space. Due to the low performance of embedded processors, this method is not suitable for dealing with modern multi process concurrent communication tasks [17].

Recently, event-driven hardware aggregation operations have been widely used in ASIC for network. The principle is to trigger the pre-set operation or sequence of events by user-predefined triggering events to complete the complex communication mode. This method requires host nodes to prepare the set of operations in advance and deliver them to the hardware structure. Additional mechanisms are needed to ensure that activated event is earlier than the triggering event, before all processes are ready [17]. If unexpected messages are received, the host processor intervention is required. These limitations and additional overhead reduce the performance advantage of the hardware collection operation [18].

## 2.3  Conclusion

To sum up, collective communications play an important role in improving the computational efficiency of modern high-performance computer systems. The collective communications dealing with small amount of data cannot be improved by software implementation efficiently due to the communication delay. Hence, hardware implementation is more suitable to optimize delay. Hardware implementation requires additional mechanism and overhead to control communication because of the uncertain number of processes, and moreover scalability remains the primary problem for hardware implementation.

# 3  RBPCCM

## 3.1  Serialism and Parallelism of Collective Communications

Programs are distributed in a number of processes to work simultaneously in the parallel system. These processes, which work in different computational endpoints, demand for the block collective communication to transfer data and control. Sometimes, programs take part in the communications among processes. These communications are irrelative and thus can be performed simultaneously. Besides, the collective communications among jobs can be executed parallel if they are irrelative. The illustration of the collective communication for the parallel programs is shown as following:

The Virtual Collective ID (VCID) is used to manage the collective communications for multi-process jobs in RBPCCM. The VCID is consisted by the following three elements.

• Communication ID (CMID)

The ID of collective communications for parallel programs: used for distinguishing the execution phases of programs.

• Iteration Number (LN)

The iteration number for collective communications: representing the iterative execution number for the non-relax order collective communications.

• Collective Resource Allocation number (CRA)

Core resources for RBPCCM: the collective communications with the same CRA are treated as the non-relax order communications, while the communications with different CRAs can be performed parallel.

The collective communication in Fig. 1 is organized to be the communication sequences shown in Fig. 2 by using VCID. The three-section numbers in Fig. 2 represent {CMID-LN-CRA}. The non-relax communications in part1 of Fig. 2(a) all have the $0^{th}$ CRA. Therefore, the first communication with the $0^{th}$ CRA as well is blocked and cannot be executed until all communications in part1 are finished. However, the other communications in part2 are capable to be performed parallel since they are distributed to different CRAs, after part1 is over.

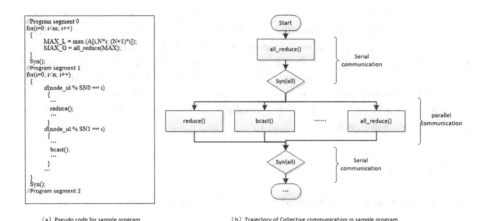

(a) Pseudo code for sample program    (b) Trajectory of Collective communication in sample program

**Fig. 1.** Examples of serial and parallel collective communication in parallel programs

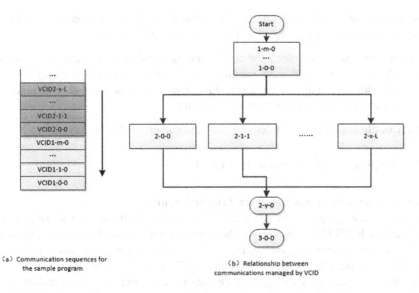

(a) Communication sequences for the sample program

(b) Relationship between communications managed by VCID

**Fig. 2.** Collective communication sequence for program in Fig. 1

## 3.2 Processes for Collective Communications

The computational endpoints are distributed by the job management system in reality [19], and software only need to focus on the relations among processes. Hence, RBPCCM constructs the virtual collective communication tree by software, and implements collective communications by hardware. The virtual collective communication tree breaks the physics restriction for interconnect network, so it is commonly used in collective communications through software implementation. An example of collective communication tress is illustrated in Fig. 3.

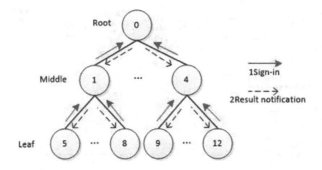

**Fig. 3.** Processing flow of collective communication

The hardware complexity is reduced and the implementation of offload collective communications is also benefitted by optimizing the processes for collective communications. Hardware optimizes the procedures of the three collective communications into two steps in the virtual tress constructed by software.

**Sign in:** Each endpoint collects the corresponding sign-in communications from its all son endpoints firstly, and then submitted the sign-in communication to its father endpoint. The root endpoint initializes the gather notifications to all endpoints after receiving all sign-in communications successfully.

**Result notification:** CPU is informed after the gather result is received.

### 3.3   Hardware Acceleration of RBPCCM

**Sign-in Communications Based on Trigger Events.**
Descriptors are generated by software according to applications, and submitted to hardware in RBPCCM mechanism. The configuration information of the virtual collective communication tree, such as the number of the son endpoints and order of father endpoints, are included in the descriptors of collective communication.
The brief structure of RBPCCM is demonstrated in Fig. 7. CRA pending Buffer (CRA_BUF) and VCID matching unit are the key components. CRA_BUF is designed for storing the processing information, and controlling the parallel execution of collective communications. VCID_MU is responsible for matching descriptors and the packets received from the network, processing legal communication request and responding error notification for the illegal requests (Fig. 4).

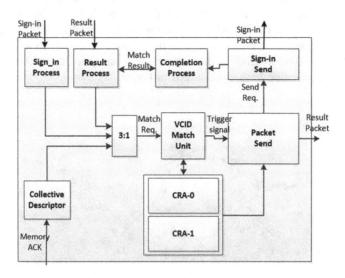

**Fig. 4.** The structure sign-in unit

VCID, father ID, son sequence, etc., are contained in the sign-in network packets; the complete information about collective communications is included in the collective descriptors. CRA resource is operated after receiving sign-in network packets and descriptors. The related information including VCID is written if CRA is valid. Otherwise VCID is matched and then the related information is written to CRA_BUF.

The trigger conditions and events for CRA are illustrated in Table 1. RBPCCM automatically finishes the process of collective communication according to the status and trigger conditions of CRA.

**Table 1.** Triggered events of CRA

| CRA status | Endpoint type | Trigger condition | Trigger event |
|---|---|---|---|
| Sign-in status | Son | Submitting descriptors | Sending the sign-in network packets to its father endpoints |
| | Middle | Collecting the sign-in packets from all son endpoints | |
| | Root | Collecting the sign-in packets from all son endpoints | Sending the gather result packets |
| Result notifications | Son | Receiving the gather result packets matching VCID | Informing CPU according to the gather results |
| | Middle | | |
| | Root | | |

**Optimization for Result Notifications.**
All endpoints involved in collective communications are prepared for receiving result notifications after the phase of sign-in communication is over. In nature, the phase of gather results is the one-to-many communication process. RBPCCM supports two approaches to improve this phase.

Hierarchical parallel communications based on the virtual tree: The result notifications are sent from father endpoints to son endpoints hierarchy by hierarchy according to the information recorded in CRA, opposite to the direction of sign-in communications.

One-to-many communications: Root endpoint performs the one-to-many communication to all endpoints to notify the gather results.

VCID is required in gather result packets. CRAs in the phase of gather result match VCID, and then, if succeed, process gather results according to descriptors and release CRAs after notifying CPU.

## 4   Verification of RBPCCM

### 4.1   Scalability Verification

Sunway Taihu Light is a petascale super computer for large scale parallel processing, composed of 40960 compute nodes, which is deployed in the National Supercomputing Center in Wuxi. We build the functional model for the RBPCCM in the Sunway Taihu Light compute system, and then conduct experiments on different nodes set, such as 256,5000,10000 and other node sizes, which constructed kinds of virtual set tree structures. Finally, we complete the tests of collective communication types such as barrier synchronization, reduce, all reduce, multicast and broadcast.

The experimental results show that the RBPCCM uses VCID to manage the set communication in a unified way, which simplifies the serial and concurrent control processes between different sets of communications. The method, with better scalability, based on the virtual set tree can be free from be affected directly by the network topology architecture, but also can be flexibly applied to the communication of different interconnection modes and node sizes.

## 4.2 Design and Implementation of RBPCCM Prototype Chip

The Virtex7 XC2000T chip of Xilinx is selected and the FPGA verification system of RBPCCM prototype chip is constructed based on it. The system consists of four prototype chips and one tile-scale router system Rout1. Each RBPCCM prototype chip is connected with the x86 server through the PCIe interface. The operating frequency of the FPGA system is 2.4 MHz, while the x86 server is 2.6 GHz (Fig. 5).

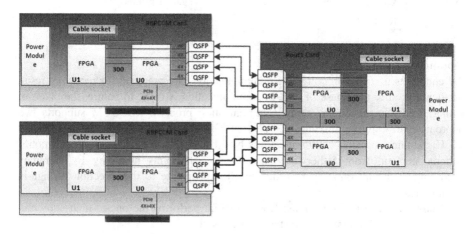

**Fig. 5.** FPGA verification system architecture

# 5 Performance Testing and Analysis of RBPCCM

## 5.1 Testing Condition

The performance test of RBPCCM is carried out on the FPGA verification system. Based on the point-to-point communication in the prototype chip, a standard MPI (Message Passing Interface) is implemented. The CCI (Collective Communication Interface) is implemented according to the RBPCCM. Two classes of communication test problems of blocking and non-blocking are designed. Then, MPI and CCI are called for actual running test. Each test cycle is run 10000 times. Finally, the average test results are calculated and compared (Table 2).

**Table 2.** Collective communication test items

| Title | Description | |
| --- | --- | --- |
| syn | Blocking | Based on the realization of the synchronization barrier; |
| isyn | Non-blocking | executing with blocking |
| reduce | Blocking | Double precision floating-point addition calculation; the |
| ireduce | Non-blocking | amount of data is 2 KB; only root process save the result data |
| bcast | Blocking | Data multicast operations; root processes send 2 KB data to |
| ibcast | Non-blocking | all other processes |
| all_reduce | Blocking | Double precision floating-point addition operation; the |
| iall_reduce | Non-blocking | amount of data is 2 KB; all processes receive the result data |

On the test scale, each RBPCCM supports 16 processes, and the FPGA verification system has four RBPCCM chips, with the capability of supporting 64 nodes of the virtual set communication tree. The performance of collective communications under different process scales is tested on the cases of 4, 8, 16, 32, 64 processes.

Due to the great difference between the running frequency of FPGA system and the host CPU, the absolute delay information is meaningless. Therefore, the comparison parameter is designed based on the result using the MPI test delay divided by the CCI test delay, in order to calculate the acceleration performance of RBPCCM.

$$\text{Speedup} = \text{TMPI/TCCI} \tag{1}$$

## 5.2   Test Result and Analysis

The CCI speedup column diagram of the 8 test programs is shown in Fig. 6.

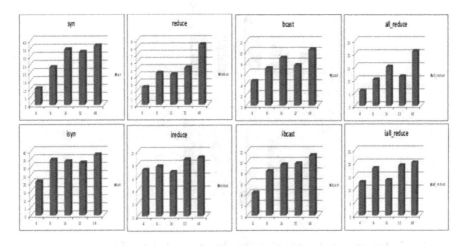

**Fig. 6.** Comparison of acceleration effects in different process scales

As shown in the above figure, all the CCI communication test acceleration rates are greater than 1. The hardware collective communication of RBPCCM has obvious acceleration effect, with the acceleration ratio scale from 2 to 34, and the average speedup ratio of 9 times.

In the barrier synchronization operation, CCI achieved the best acceleration performance, which maximum acceleration ratio can reach 34 times. The reason is that there is no fence synchronization calculation or data mobile operation in CCI mode, each node in a synchronous operation only need to send one description to the RBPCCM, and hardware take full offload way to complete the entire communication operation. In contrast, the MPI uses point-to-point communication to achieve the synchronization message, so each node needs to launch multiple communications, and the Host processor is required to do interventional treatment each time.

It is shown that the reduce communication has the worst improvement only between 2 and 5 times. There are two reasons: the first is the characteristic of reduce communication. The implication of reduce communication is that only the root node needs the result data, and the other sub nodes can exit after completing the sign-in communication. In RBPCCM, all the collective communication processes are unified as the two fixed phase, sign-in and result notification, so the sub nodes, which don't need the results, also have to wait until the results arrive to complete communication. The second reason is that data computing is done by the host processor in MPI mode. From the previous section, we know that in our FPGA environment, the host processor runs at much higher frequency than the FPGA system, 2.6 GHz vs. 2.4 MHz. In real environments, the performance gap between RBPCCM and host processor is not so large, so the result should be better than the current test.

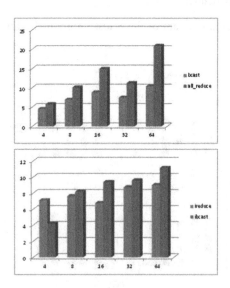

**Fig. 7.** Comparison of acceleration times between ALL_REDUCE and BCAST

As shown in Fig. 7, the speedup of ALL_REDUCE is higher than BCAST operation in most cases. The data needs to be calculated and processed for ALL_REDUCE; even these two communications are similar. It is demonstrated that the acceleration improvement is obvious due to RBPCCM working in offload mode, although the host processor runs much faster than FPGA in the FPGA verification system.

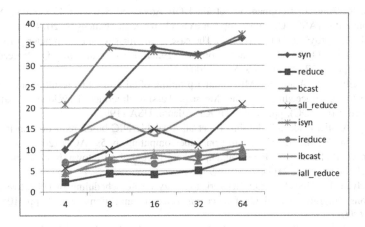

**Fig. 8.** Acceleration multiple curves under different number process

Figure 8 illustrates the acceleration times for each test subject in different scales of process. It can be seen from the diagram that, as the number of processes increases, the speedup of RBPCCM tends to keep increasing. It also shows that, when dealing with small amount of data, as the number of processes that participate in collective communication increases, the speedup of the implementation based on software algorithm is reduced.

## 6    Conclusion and Future Work

This paper studies the collective communication based on hardware, and proposes a scalable hardware collective communication mechanism RBPCCM. RBPCCM is verified in the Sunway Taihu Light computing system. We implemented RBPCCM in the network interface chip, and built the FPGA verification system for performance test. The proposed method is proven to be able to accelerate 2.4–37 times, and the average acceleration is 14 times, compared with the collective communication based on point-to-point message in 64 processes.

Limited by the experimental conditions, the test of RBPCCM is only performed in the 64 process scale FPGA system. In addition, the RBPCCM mechanism implemented in this paper supports broadcast and reduce operations, in which the maximum amount of data is 2048 bytes. Future work will continue to study the hardware collective communication mechanisms for larger scale data.

Finally, thanks to Yu Kang, Chen Shuping and others for help and support of this work.

**Acknowledgements.** This research is supported by National Science and Technology Major Project with No. 2013ZX0102-8001-001-001.

# References

1. Lucas, R., Ang, J., Bergman, K., et al.: DOE Advanced Scientific Computing Advisory Subcommittee (ASCAC) report: top ten exascale research challenges (2014)
2. Petrini, F., Kerbyson, D.J., Pakin, S.: The case of the missing supercomputer performance. In: Achieving Optimal Performance on the 8192 Processors of ASCI Q, Proceedings of SC2003, pp. 1–17. ACM, New York (2003)
3. Rabenseifner, R.: Automatic MPI counter profiling of all users: first result on a CRAY T3E 900-512. In: Proceedings of the Message Passing Interface Developer's and User's Conference (MPIDC), pp. 77–85. HLRS, Atlanta, USA (1999)
4. Moody, A., Fernandez, J., Petrini, F., et al.: Scalable NIC-based reduction on large-scale clusters. In: ACM/IEEE Conference on Supercomputing, p. 59. ACM (2003)
5. Culler, D., Richard, K.Y., Patterson, D., Eicken, T. et al.: LogP: towards a realistic model of parallel computation. **28**(7), 1–12 (1993)
6. Gabrielyan, E., Hersch, R.D.: Network topology aware scheduling of collective communications. In: International Conference on Telecommunications, vol. 2, pp. 1051–1058. IEEE (2003)
7. Sanders, P., Sibeyn, J.F.: A bandwidth latency tradeoff for broadcast and reduction. In: Bode, A., Ludwig, T., Karl, W., Wismüller, R. (eds.) Euro-Par 2000. LNCS, vol. 1900, pp. 918–926. Springer, Heidelberg (2000). https://doi.org/10.1007/3-540-44520-X_128
8. Hoefler, T., Squyres, J.M., Rehm, W., Lumsdaine, A.: A case for non-blocking collective operations. In: Min, G., Di Martino, B., Yang, L.T., Guo, M., Rünger, G. (eds.) ISPA 2006. LNCS, vol. 4331, pp. 155–164. Springer, Heidelberg (2006). https://doi.org/10.1007/11942634_17
9. Petrini, F., Coll, S., Frachtenberg, E., et al.: Hardware- and software-based collective communication on the quadrics network. In: IEEE International Symposium on Network Computing and Applications, pp. 24–35. IEEE (2001)
10. Giampapa, M.E., Giampapa, M.E., Giampapa, M.E., et al.: The deep computing messaging framework: generalized scalable message passing on the blue gene/P supercomputer. International Conference on Supercomputing, pp. 94–103. ACM (2008)
11. Faraj, A., Kumar, S., Smith, B., et al.: MPI collective communications on the Blue Gene/P supercomputer: algorithms and optimizations. In: International Conference on Supercomputing, pp. 489–490. ACM (2009)
12. Haring, R., Ohmacht, M., Fox, T., et al.: The IBM Blue Gene/Q compute chip. IEEE Micro **32**(2), 48–60 (2011)
13. Arimilli, B., Arimilli, R., Chung, V., et al.: The PERCS high-performance interconnect, pp. 75–82. IEEE (2010)
14. Mai, L., Rupprecht, L., Alim, A., et al.: NetAgg: using middleboxes for application-specific on-path aggregation in data centres, vol. 23(6), pp. 249–262 (2014)
15. Wagner, A., Jin, H.W., Panda, D.K., et al.: NIC-based offload of dynamic user-defined modules for Myrinet clusters. IEEE International Conference on CLUSTER Computing, pp. 205–214. IEEE Computer Society (2004)
16. Yu, W., Buntinas, D., Graham, R.L., et al.: Efficient and scalable barrier over quadrics and Myrinet with a new NIC-based collective message passing protocol, p. 182 (2004)

17. Zahavi, E., Zahavi, E., Zahavi, E., et al.: Scalable hierarchical aggregation protocol (SHArP): a hardware architecture for efficient data reduction. In: The Workshop on Optimization of Communication in HPC, pp. 1–10. IEEE Press (2016)

18. Arap, O., Swany, M.: Offloading collective operations to programmable logic on a Zynq cluster. In: High-Performance Interconnects, pp. 76–83. IEEE (2016)

19. Lu, Y., Shen, Z., Zhou, E., Zhu, M.: MCRM system: CIM-. In: Chen, G., Pan, Y., Guo, M., Lu, J. (eds.) ISPA 2005. LNCS, vol. 3759, pp. 549–558. Springer, Heidelberg (2005). https://doi.org/10.1007/11576259_60

# Experiment and Finite Element Analysis of Stochastic Vibration of Severe Environment Computer

Jihong Jian, Cunxian Cao$^{(\boxtimes)}$, Xianpei Luo, and Qianqian Yang

The Computer Department, Jiangsu Automation Research Institute,
Lianyungang, China
jjhjian@126.com, ccx1237@126.com, lxp8212@163.com,
yqq1203@126.com

**Abstract.** The stochastic vibration Experiment is the basic requirement in the reinforcement of the severe computer resistance test. In this paper, the finite element model of the computer is established and the validity of the model is verified by free modal analysis. The modal solution, stress distribution and acceleration power spectral density (PSD) are obtained by modal analysis and stochastic dynamics analysis of the finite element model. The acceleration response of the structure is obtained by stochastic vibration experiment, and the acceleration PSD curve of the structure is obtained by Fourier transform. By comparison, it is found that the error of resonant frequency at the corresponding point obtained by simulation and experiment is less than 10%, and the accuracy is reasonable. Dynamic simulation based on stochastic vibration experiment can shorten the development period of the product and play an important role in product optimization and fault diagnosis.

**Keywords:** Stochastic vibration · Resistance harsh environment computer
Power spectral density (PSD) · Model test

## 1 Introduction

Severe environment Computer is an important part of shipboard equipment and systems, which subjects to the ship's stochastic vibration load in working, so it is necessary to ensure its stiffness and strength to meet the requirements in the structural design [1]. The anti-vibration designs of electronic equipment mainly rely on experience and the final identification experiment to ensure, which results that the product development process often needs to be repeated several times. In the early stage of product design, the method of finite element analysis can simulate the behavior of the severe environment computer, which can guide product design, greatly shorten the product development cycle and reduce costs [2].

In this paper, the finite element analysis is used to simulate the stochastic vibration experiment of the severe environment computer. The precision of the finite element simulation is analyzed by experiment. Finally, the guidance of the product design is given according to the results of finite element simulation.

© Springer Nature Singapore Pte Ltd. 2018
W. Xu et al. (Eds.): NCCET 2017, CCIS 600, pp. 76–85, 2018.
https://doi.org/10.1007/978-981-10-7844-6_8

## 2  Stochastic Dynamics Theory and Experiment

### 2.1  Stochastic Dynamics Theory

A multi-degree-of-freedom system with a concentrated parameter is subjected to an excitation from the base, and its equation of motion can be expressed as [3]:

$$M\ddot{x} + C\dot{x} + Kx = c\{e\}u + K\{e\}u \qquad (1)$$

where $M$ is the system mass matrix, $C$ is the system damping matrix, $K$ is the system stiffness matrix, $\{e\}$ is the unit column vector, $u$ is the basis of acceleration, $x$ is the degree of freedom of the acceleration response.

The frequency response characteristic vector is marked as $G_x(\omega)$. $S_x(\omega)$ is the degree of freedom of the power spectral density function vector. Let $u(t) = e^{i\omega t}$, $x(t) = G_x(\omega)e^{i\omega t}$, then Eq. (1) can be derived as Eq. (2):

$$(K - M\omega^2 + i\omega C)G_x(\omega) = (K + i\omega C)\{e\} \qquad (2)$$

With the regular transformations $G_x(\omega) = \phi Z_x(\omega)$, $G_x(\omega)$ can be expressed as:

$$G_x(\omega) = \phi H(\omega)\phi^T(K + i\omega C)\{e\} \qquad (3)$$

where $H(\omega) = diag[1/(\omega_t^2 - \omega^2 + 2j\omega\omega_t)]$, $G_x(\omega)$ is an n-dimensional vector, its jth component can be marked as $G_{xj}(\omega)$. According to the stochastic excitation-response relation, the corresponding power spectral density $S_{xj}(\omega)$ of the respective degrees of freedom can be expressed as follows:

$$S_{xj}(\omega) = \left|G_{xj}(\omega)^2\right|^2 S_u(\omega) \qquad (4)$$

The mean square of the response is:

$$x_j^2 = \int_{-\infty}^{+\infty} S_{xj}(\omega)d\omega \qquad (5)$$

Therefore, the response of the acceleration power spectral density is $S_{\ddot{x}j}(\omega)$:

$$S_{\ddot{x}j}(\omega) = \omega^4 S_{xj}(\omega) \qquad (6)$$

### 2.2  Stochastic Dynamics Experiment

The vibration experiment system consists of three parts: control acquisition system, power amplifier and vibration table. The control acquisition system transmits the experiment load to the power amplifier with the small signal of the alternating current, and then drives the vibration table movement through the amplification of the signal, and controls the acquisition system to continuously collect the response of the vibration.

The severe environment computer in the direction of the three axes is tested in accordance with the value of Fig. 1 [4].

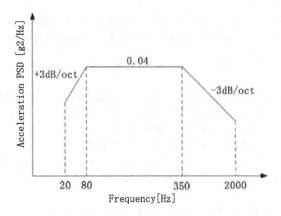

**Fig. 1.** Stochastic vibration spectrum

# 3   Numerical Calculation and Analysis

## 3.1   Finite Element Model of Severe Environment Computer

### 3.1.1   Finite Element Model for Severe Environment Computer

Severe environment computer consists of the frame structure, front and rear panels, PCB, fins, fans, filters, plug-in modules and other components. The geometric model is shown in Fig. 2.

According to the working condition and force of the harsh environment, the geometric model is simplified firstly. In order to reduce the calculation scale and improve the computational efficiency, the geometric features of the original geometric model with little influence on the analysis result are removed, such as chamfering, fillet and non-mounting connections in the model. However, considering the phenomenon of the stress concentration occurs in the screw hole edge connector, the screw connection is reserved, which is established in the microscopic modeling.

With ICEM CFD, the grid is simplified for the severe environment computer. In order to describe the structure of the acceleration and stress response more accurately, the chassis of other structures are used hexahedral structure grid (solid185) in addition to corrugated board, and to ensure that the structure of the thin wall contains more than three layers of element, corrugated board are used the quadrilateral mesh (shell181). Finally, the entire grid model is assembled as shown in Fig. 3.

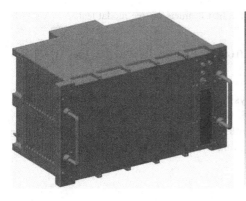 

**Fig. 2.** Geometric model of severe environment computer

**Fig. 3.** Grid model of severe environment computer

### 3.1.2   Model Test

Before the analysis of the finite element model, it is necessary to test the validity of the model to ensure the correctness of the model and avoid the invalid result and the convergence. In this part, two kinds of validity test methods commonly used in mechanical finite element analysis are selected as follows:

(1)   Test of quality characteristics

After the finite element model established in ANSYS, the element properties of the model can be selected to obtain the finite element quality characteristics of the structure in the output window. The quality characteristics of each type of element are as follows:

**Table 1.** Quality characteristics of each type of element

| Element type | Solid185 | Shell181 | Mass21 | Total |
|---|---|---|---|---|
| Quantity | 634417 | 61824 | 2 | 696243 |
| Mass/kg | 18.1115 | 2.9600 | 0.2354 | 21.3069 |

While the actual measured mass is 22.6 kg, the error is only 5.7%. It can be seen that the finite element model is close to quality of the actual structure, the error mainly comes from the internal cable of the chassis. The finite element model has a good simulation effect on the actual structure in terms of quality characteristics.

(2)   Free modal test

Free modal test is an important method in finite element analysis. The test method can determine whether there are redundant constraints and insufficient constraints in the finite element model.

The basic constraint in the finite element model is removed and the modal analysis is carried out. The first 8 order modal frequencies obtained by the Block Lanczos are shown in Table 2 below:

**Table 2.** Natural frequencies of the first 8 orders of free modal test

| Orders | 1 | 2 | 3 | 4 | 5 | 6 | 7 | 8 |
|---|---|---|---|---|---|---|---|---|
| Frequency/Hz | 0.00125 | 0.00137 | 0.00173 | 0.00195 | 0.00229 | 0.00237 | 11.784 | 31.924 |

From the results of the free modal analysis, we can see that the natural frequency of the first 6 orders is relatively close to zero, which indicates that there is no redundant constraint in the structure. And the 7th-order frequency is 11.784 Hz, which is the 1st-order natural frequency of the structure, that is to say there is no case of insufficient constraint.

## 3.2  Modal Analysis

The finite element model of the severe environment computer with the boundary conditions is shown in Fig. 4.

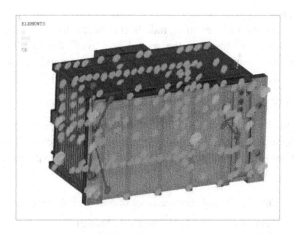

**Fig. 4.** Finite element model of severe environment computer

In the case of the boundary conditions shown in Fig. 4, the modal analysis of the finite element model in ANSYS and the expansion and extraction of the first 6 order frequencies using the Block Lanczos method are shown in Table 3 below:

**Table 3.** Severe environment of the first eight bands of the natural frequency

| Orders | Frequency/Hz | Mode describe |
|---|---|---|
| 1 | 11.79 | Scaleboard X to a bend |
| 2 | 35.29 | Scaleboard X to the second bend |
| 3 | 128.54 | Integer X to a bend |
| 4 | 192.20 | Integer X to the second bend |
| 5 | 207.24 | PCB X to a bend |
| 6 | 215.37 | Integer X to twist |

The first 6 orders modes are extracted as shown in Fig. 5:

(a) 1st order

(b) 2nd order

(c) 3rd order

(d) 4th order

(e) 5th order

(f) 6th order

**Fig. 5.** Modes of severe environment computer

From the results of the above modal analysis, it can be seen that the majority of modes of severe environment computer are local modes, and the modes are distributed on some local parts of the structure. From the natural frequency in Table 3, we can see that the frequency of the first 2 orders is low, the vibration mode mainly occurs at the lining of the filter and the scaleboard, where the stiffness is weak because the connection between the scaleboard and the frame point along the Y and Z direction to the distribution of the distance. It is recommended to reduce the size of the scaleboard here in order to provide sufficient normal stiffness.

### 3.3  Stochastic Dynamics Analysis

#### 3.3.1  Acceleration PSD Correspondence and Error Analysis

The damping coefficient of the structure is 0.05. Since the frequency range of the load spectrum excitation is 20 Hz–2000 Hz and the mode is dense, it is necessary to extract enough orders of the finite element model of the severe environment computer to ensure the accuracy of the results [5]. 150 modal orders are taken into the participation of the calculation to ensure the coverage of the frequency range of excitation [6].

In the ANSYS, a stochastic dynamic analysis method (Spectrum) is used to obtain the acceleration response of the stiffener. The Fourier transform is used to convert the time domain data to the frequency domain data and calculate the structural acceleration PSD response. Take a point on the right side of the severe environment Wall, scaleboard, PCB and backplane to extract the acceleration PSD response respectively. The comparison of results of the finite element analysis and experiment are shown in Fig. 6.

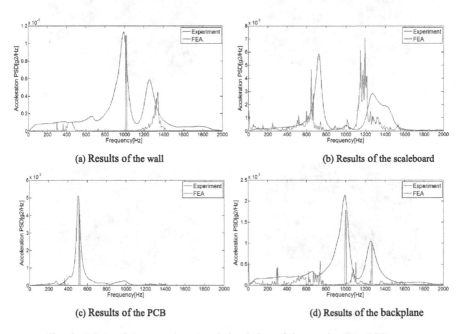

(a) Results of the wall

(b) Results of the scaleboard

(c) Results of the PCB

(d) Results of the backplane

**Fig. 6.** Points of the experiment and simulation of the acceleration PSD curve

It can be seen from Fig. 6 that the results of the stochastic dynamics analysis are close to the acceleration PSD response modes and values obtained by the experiment. From the frequency of the maximum values of the acceleration PSD, it can be seen that the maximum values of the acceleration PSD of the four components do not appear at the lower order frequency because the lower order modes of the structure are local modal, the vibration response is small. Therefore, even if the structure of the first few modal frequency is small, the stochastic load on the structure of the impact is not significant.

The maximum value of the acceleration PSD $(X10^{-3}(m/s^2)^2/Hz)$ and the corresponding frequency (Hz) are shown in Table 4.

**Table 4.** Acceleration PSD, corresponding frequency and error analysis of experiment and FEA

| Component | Maximal acceleration PSD frequency (FEA) | Maximal acceleration PSD frequency (Experiment) | Relative error |
|---|---|---|---|
| PCB | 0.0051/505 | 0.0047/515 | 8.51%/ 1.94% |
| Scaleboard | 0.0049/710 | 0.0047/650 | 4.25%/ 9.23% |
| Wall | 0.0011/991 | 0.0010/1015 | 10.00%/ 2.36% |
| Backplane | 0.0019/991 | 0.0018/1000 | 5.56%/ 0.9% |

In contrast, the frequency that the maximum acceleration PSD occurred in of PCB and scaleboard is smaller than its of wall and backplane. Because the modulus and stiffness of the PCB is small and scaleboard is due to the high-mass of the filter results in a smaller local mode. Therefore, more attention should be placed on the design of scaleboard and installation of the filter. In addition, the maximum value of the acceleration PSD of PCB and scaleboard is also relatively large.

### 3.3.2  Stress and Strength Analysis
The stochastic vibration analysis of the severe environment computer was carried out, and the following calculation results were obtained. Table 5 shows the $3\sigma$ solution of

**Table 5.** The $3\sigma$ solution of the stress response of the computer under stochastic vibration.

| Components | X to the vibration stress (MPa) | Y to the vibration stress (MPa) | Z to the vibration stress (MPa) | Strength limit (MPa) | Safety factor |
|---|---|---|---|---|---|
| Framework structure | 28.2 | 49.2 | 93.6 | 270 | 2.88 |
| Backplane and PCB | 17.1 | 28.4 | 7.35 | 338.4 | >10 |
| Fan hood, bracket, holder | 92.4 | 36.9 | 71.4 | 780 | 8.44 |
| Front and rear covers, panels | 72.3 | 31.5 | 222.6 | 390 | 5.39 |
| Fan | 36.3 | 19.4 | 0.72 | 100 | 2.75 |
| Motherboard Modules | 45.9 | 8.7 | 1.53 | 390 | 8.49 |

the stress response of the various components of the computer under stochastic vibration.

In view of the high level of stress in the Z-direction stochastic vibration of the computer, in order to check whether the strength of its key components meets the requirements, Fig. 7 shows the stress diagram of frame structure of the material classification, front and rear covers and panels, fan hoods, brackets and fixed frame and the PCB and other major structural parts.

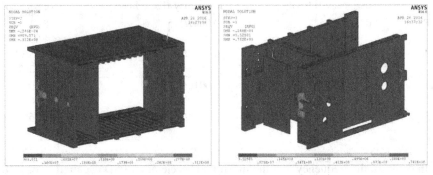

(a) Stress diagram of frame structure    (b) Stress diagram of front and rear cover and panel

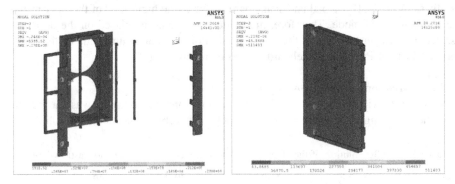

(c) Stress diagram of steel           (d) Stress diagram of board module

**Fig. 7.** Stress diagram of the main parts of the computer

It can be seen from the figure that the $3\sigma$ value of the stress response of the computer under stochastic vibration is 222.6 MPa, which is caused by the bolt hole connected to the rear cover and the frame. Therefore, considering the larger weight of the rear cover, it is recommended to add a bolt connection point at the maximum stress point symmetrically to increase the local strength of the connection further and reduce the maximum stress in the design of the structure. In terms of probability, it can be considered that the probability is 99.73% that the maximum value of structural stress response is less than 222.6 MPa [7], which meet the structural strength requirements.

# 4 Conclusion

From the finite element simulation and experimental analysis of the severe environment, the following conclusions are obtained:

(1) Resonant frequency error of the acceleration power spectral density of the corresponding point obtained by simulation and experiment is less than 10%, and the accuracy is reasonable.
(2) The maximum value of the acceleration PSD of the components of the computer does not appear at the lower order frequency because the lower order modes of the structures are local modal; the overall vibration response is small.
(3) The frequency of the first 2 orders is low, the vibration mode mainly occurs at the lining of the filter and the scaleboard, where the stiffness is weak because the connection between the scaleboard and the frame point along the Y and Z direction to the distribution of the distance. It is recommended to reduce the size of the scaleboard here in order to provide sufficient normal stiffness.
(4) The $3\sigma$ value of the stress response of the computer under stochastic vibration is 222.6 MPa, it can be considered that the probability is 99.73% that the maximum value of structural stress response is less than 222.6 MPa.

# References

1. Jinghui, C.: Construct collectivity design of ship borne electronic equipment. J. Ship Electr. Eng. **26**(2), 163–166 (2006)
2. Lei, H.: A certain type of structural design of reinforced mainframe computer chassis. J. Mech. Manag. Dev. **22**(5), 7–9 (2010)
3. Liang, Z., Xu, D., Li, Y., Chen, T.: Random vibration analysis of mounting rack for helicopeter borne equipment. J. Electro-Mech. Eng. **25**(5), 21–24 (2009)
4. Zheng, Z., Wang, Y.: Introduction of parameters in random vibration and their calculation. J. Electr. Prod. Reliab. Environ. Test. **27**(6), 45–48 (2009)
5. Liu, Z., Guo, J., Yang, L.: Random vibration analysis of airborne electronic equipment structure. J. Aeronaut. Comput. Tech. **41**(4), 91–93 (2011)
6. Yong, Z., Ma, L., Liu, S., et al.: The coupling effects of thermal cycling and high current density on Sn58Bi solder joints. J. Mater. Sci. **48**(6), 2318–2325 (2013)
7. Wang, Q., Chen, M.: Emulation and analysis of random vibration. Electro-optic Technol. Appl. **24**(5), 77–80 (2009)

# Integrated Protection Design of an Anti-harsh Environment Reinforcement Chassis

Miao Zhang[✉], Daoqing Qu, Jiangfeng Huang,
and Shangyong Liang

The Computer Department, Jiangsu Automation Research Institute,
Lianyungang, China
zm86325@126.com, {qudaoqing,huangjiangfeng,
liangshangyong}@jari.cn

**Abstract.** As the main content of structural design for electronic equipment, chassis design has become an important part to achieve technical indicators. The paper discusses design ideas of an anti-harsh environment reinforcement chassis deeply, and describes particularly thermal design, electromagnetic compatibility design, anti-vibration and anti-impact design and so on. The methods and main structure diagram are given in each part of the design in this paper. The anti-harsh environment reinforcement chassis is taken environmental tests to make sure that it has good reliability and integrated protection capabilities, which provides a reference for similar engineering design.

**Keywords:** Reinforcement chassis · Integrated protection
Environmental tests · Reliability

## 1 Introduction

Chassis plays an important role in the life and work efficiency of electronic equipment, which makes sure the safety and stabilization of electronic components [1]. As modern military electronic equipment used in high-tech products, it is not only to meet equipment function, but also to meet the environmental requirements of the equipment. A well designed electronic chassis is the basis of improving the reliability of the modern electronic equipment, which can withstand the strong vibration shock and electromagnetic interference, as well as the harsh weather conditions [2, 3]. With the rapid development of electronic information, the performance of the anti-harsh environment computer is getting higher and higher. Therefore, the existing reinforcement computer has been unable to meet the cooling requirements of multiple high-performance main modules. The paper introduces an anti-harsh environment chassis, which elaborates the chassis design, thermal design, electromagnetic compatibility design, anti-vibration and anti-impact design and so on.

W. Xu et al. (Eds.): NCCET 2017, CCIS 600, pp. 86–95, 2018.
https://doi.org/10.1007/978-981-10-7844-6_9

## 2  Chassis Structure Design

As shown in Fig. 1, the reinforcement chassis is with five independent air ducts that are connected to the inlet and outlet. First of all, the ducts use a rectangular corrugated board. High-performance main modules are cooled by cold plate which is fit through the thermal pad and the side wall closely. It increases the heat dissipation area of each cooling channel and shortens the heat path. Then, it strengthens the fit of the cold plate with the side wall of the air duct through wedge locking device, which improves thermal efficiency. And then the high-power fan is used to pump air, which ensures every main module to be cooled through own independent air duct. High performance electrical connectors in the rear cover of the chassis are welded to signal transfer board. And main modules are inserted into the Compact Peripheral Component Interconnect socket of the printed circuit board [4]. The signal transfer board is connected to the printed circuit board through a flexible printed circuit board, which avoids compatibility between cables.

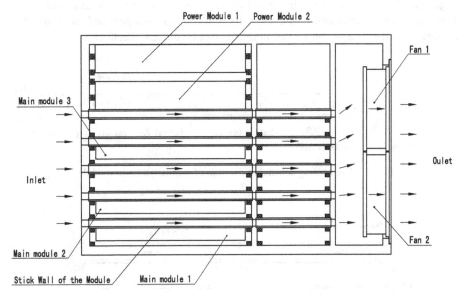

**Fig. 1.** The schematic diagram of multi-ducts cooling chassis

## 3  Thermal Design

### 3.1  Framework Design

In order to ensure that the reinforcement computer in a harsh environment can be stable and reliable work, it needs to takes the chassis to strengthen the fully enclosed structure. Five parallel ducts and corrugated boards are weld in the chassis through the vacuum brazing process, which can ensure that external ducts are isolated from internal modules and the printed circuit board. The technology of vacuum brazing can make the

88    M. Zhang et al.

framework heat evenly and have small deformation. Furthermore, the vertical and parallelism of the board is good. The chassis framework is made of rust-proof aluminum plate because of its low density, corrosion resistance, high thermal conductivity and good electrical conductivity, which can improve the natural heat dissipation capacity of the chassis.

### 3.2 Cold Plate Design

The heat of the chassis is mainly from the components of the module, so it is the key to make it heat to the air. Figure 2 shows heat dissipation diagram of the traditional main module. The heat of components transfers through the thermal pad to the cold plate, and then conducts to the chassis slot board. Finally, the heat is forced to the outside of the chassis through ducts on the slab. It is designed to have a long heat conduction path and a small thermal conductivity area. The existing main module cooling schematic diagram is shown in Fig. 3. The heat generated on the printed circuit board transfers through the thermal pad to the cold plate, and then conducts to the air duct through the large cold plate, which can put the heat of the aluminum plate out of the chassis and can also scatter the concentrated heat evenly. By reducing the heat path and increasing the cooling area, the heat of the key components can be cooled effectively.

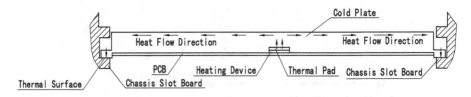

**Fig. 2.** The cooling schematic diagram of traditional main module

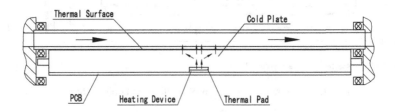

**Fig. 3.** The cooling schematic diagram of existing main module

In the process of electronic equipment cooling, the interface filler material is an important link in the thermal conduction path, which affects the overall thermal resistance of the whole heat conduction path directly. The thinner the interface filler material is, the smaller the thermal resistance is, which the better the thermal conductivity is. However, the thinner interface filler material has greater stress to electronic device in the assembly process, because the thinner interface filler material has the smaller compression deformation. But the stress between electronic devices and the cold plate in the assembly process is weakened mainly through the compression deformation of the interface filling material, it is necessary to balance the relationship between heat and external stress. In order to reduce the equivalent thermal resistance of the heating device to the cold plate, on the one hand, a new type of flexible thermal pad is select that the thermal conductivity is up to 15 (W/m·K), the other hand, the gap between heating devices and the cold plate is minimized as far as possible if the amount of compression and the stress of components are permitted.

### 3.3 Thermal Resistance Analysis

Thermal resistance is the integrated parameters to prevent the heat transfer capacity. The greater the thermal resistance is, the worse the thermal conductivity is. In a certain ambient temperature and motherboard power, the surface temperature of chips is lower in the conductive path of the small thermal resistance of. The cold plate of the main module is made up of the aluminum alloy and the heat of chips on the printed circuit board transfers to the duct shown in Fig. 3, which will encounter a variety of thermal resistance in the transmission process. The process can be analyzed in the method of electric simulation. Assumptions:

(1) Ignore heat conduction and radiation of the air gap;
(2) The thermal resistance of the thermal pad between the chip and the aluminum cold plate is equal to the one between the processor CPU and the aluminum cold plate. The size of thermal pad is 10 mm × 22 mm × 1 mm, and the thermal conductivity of pad is 15 W/(m·K).
(3) Thermal conductivity of the aluminum cold plate is 180 W/(m·K).

According to the formula $R = \delta/KA$ [5]:

$\delta_1 = 0.7 \times 10^{-3}$m, $\delta_1$ is the thickness of the CPU thermal pad after compression;
$A_1 = 15 \times 10 \times 22 \times 10^{-6}$m$^2 = 3.3 \times 10^{-3}$m$^2$, $A_1$ is the cross-sectional area of the CPU thermal pad;

$$R_1 = \delta_1/KA_1 = 0.21°C/W$$

$\delta_2 = 4 \times 10^{-3}$m, $\delta_2$ is the thickness of the aluminum plate;
$A_2 = 180 \times 135 \times 233 \times 10^{-6}$m$^2 = 5.66$ m$^2$, $A_2$ is the cross-sectional area of the aluminum cold plate;

$$R_2 = \delta_2/KA_2 = 7.06 \times 10^{-4}°C/W$$

Where $\delta$ is the thickness of the object, $A$ is the cross-sectional area perpendicular to the direction of heat conduction, $R_1$ is the thermal resistance between the chip and the aluminum cold plate, and $R_2$ is the thermal resistance of the aluminum cold plate.

In the adhesive cooling chassis, the total thermal resistance of the chip in the thermal conduction path is 2.3 °C/W.

The traditional thermal resistance is generally about 6 °C/W, obviously, in the anti-harsh environment reinforced chassis the method of adhesive heat dissipation based on ducts reduces significantly the main module chip thermal resistance, enhanced the main module external cooling capacity greatly, which solves the problem of high power dissipation.

### 3.4 Fan Selection

The heat power consumption of the reinforcement chassis is less than 300 W, according to the heat balance equation [5], the whole ventilation $Q_f$:

$$Q_f = \varphi/\rho C_p \Delta t \tag{1}$$

Where $\rho$ is the density of air, kg/m$^3$; $C_p$ is the specific heat of air, J/(kg·°C); $\varphi$ is the total loss power, W; $\Delta t$ is the temperature difference between outlet and inlet of the cooling air, °C.

The total loss power of the chassis is 300 W, the density of the air is 1.093 kg/m$^3$, the specific heat of the air is 1005 J/(kg·°C), the temperature of the cooling air inlet and the outlet is 10 °C, according to Formula (1), $Q_f = 0.027$ m$^3$/s $= 0.027 \times 35.3147$ 60 = 57.2 CFM. Taking into account the internal thermal resistance and loss of air, the required air volume is 103 CFM according to 1.8 times the redundancy design. According to the results, the main parameters of the selected axial fan are: voltage 24 VDC, power 5 W, air flow 100 CFM, wind pressure 0.28 in H$_2$O. As the chassis volume is large, and the heat should be discharged evenly, two fans are used in parallel way.

## 4 Electromagnetic Compatibility Design

Electromagnetic compatibility means that the equipment and the system can perform the coexistence of the respective functions together under the limited space, time and frequency resources [6]. Electromagnetic compatibility design is an important technical indicator of the system design of electronic equipment, and its purpose is to make the circuit module noninterference with each other, at the same time, the equipment within the system does not interfere with each other and can meet the requirements of electromagnetic compatibility.

### 4.1 Rigid and Flexible Printed Circuit Board Design

At present, the vast majority of the reinforcement chassis leads the signal line to the electrical connector by cable bundle welding, which needs to take up the larger space and is difficult to control the cable position accurately. Because of the limited chassis space and a large number of different types of cable, it will lead to electromagnetic compatibility problems interfering with each other easily. Through the technology of the flexible printed circuit board, the bottom plate is connected to the signal board to avoid electromagnetic compatibility issues caused by complex traces. As shown in

Fig. 4, the printed circuit board connectors are installed to the rigid part of the printed circuit board (signal exchange board), but do not weld, and then the electrical connectors are fixed to the chassis panel through the screws to fasten the panel and electrical connectors, and then the signal board is fixed to panel through the studs, and finally the electrical connectors are weld. The interface surface of the panel and chassis is installed with conductive rubber ropes to enhance the overall shielding effectiveness of the chassis.

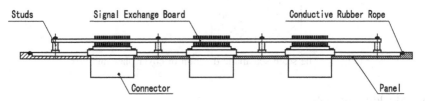

**Fig. 4.** The installation schematic diagram of connectors

## 4.2  Seams Shielding of Cover and Chassis

Shielding is an effective measure that limits the electromagnetic energy within a certain range to suppress radiation interference using conductive or magnetic materials. According to the principle of electromagnetic shielding, a seamless, non-hole and closed box has the best shielding performance [7].

The reinforcement chassis will have a combination of panels generally that cannot be contacted fully, only at some contact point, which constitutes a hole array called the seam [8]. The seam is one of the main factors that affect the shielding performance of the chassis, so it is vital importance to improve the electrical contact of these seams to the chassis design.

In order to reduce the seams of structural parts, the reinforcement chassis will be designed into a whole. Double-layer conductive rubber strips are installation on the cover of the chassis and the box (shown in Fig. 5) to ensure the electromagnetic compatibility and sealing of the chassis. It is made of silicone, silicone fluorine and other adhesives and silver, silver-plated copper and silver-plated nickel and other filler composition, which can be completed environmental seals and electromagnetic seals at the same time. Conductive rubber strips have excellent compression characteristics in a wide temperature range, which meet the US military standard wet test standard MIL-STD-810 [9]. From Fig. 5, the cover plate is fixed to the box with fastening screws, and the groove of the lower end of the screw is matched with the boss above the cover. It is provided with a flexible gasket between the groove and the boss. The contact part of the cover plate and the box is equipped with a dovetail groove for the installation of "B" type conductive rubber strip. The outer seal in the form of the whole circle is to ensure the reliability of environment sealed.

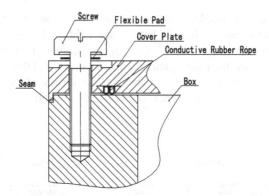

**Fig. 5.** The seam schematic diagram of cover plate and box

### 4.3    Shielding of Hole

It needs process holes to install switches, power supplies and fuses and other components in the panel, however, a metal shield covering switches and fuses can prevent electromagnetic leakage of such holes. Double-shielded structure can improve significantly the shielding effectiveness in the case of the volume of small cases that is shown in Fig. 6. An electromagnetic seal between the shield and the panel reduces the gap and improves electrical contact. A rectangular shielded socket on the side of the shield leads the switch, the fuse wire to the rectangular shield socket directly, which achieves the integration of shielded filter.

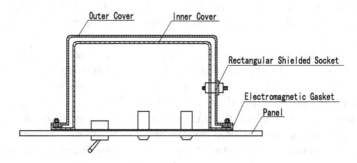

**Fig. 6.** The schematic diagram of double shield

The network port and other external interfaces on the panel are closed with a door, the contact surface of the door and the panel filled conductive shielding ropes forms a good conductor. The power cord and the signal line are wind cable shield secured connector sheath, and seams of connectors with electromagnetic shielding function and the chassis are installed conductive rubbers. Connectors, cable shield, and the chassis constitute a complete shield, effectively preventing electromagnetic interference coupled to the wire or through the installation hole into the chassis.

## 4.4   Filter and Ground

Figure 7 shows installation diagram of the filter. The power filter with a ground terminal and the signal filter are installed on both sides of the partition with screws. The electromagnetic of the chassis integrated power filter and signal filter compatibility is improved. Grounding is one of the important means of suppressing electromagnetic noise and preventing interference. For an ideal grounding system, the potential reference for each part is kept at zero potential [5]. The filter and connectors are connected to the chassis with conductive gaskets, which forms a conductor with the chassis. The cover of the chassis is equipped with a shell-mounted screw combination structure shown in Fig. 8, which is connected with ground to achieve the chassis shell ground. The contact between the screw and the panel is conductive and enhances the conductivity of it.

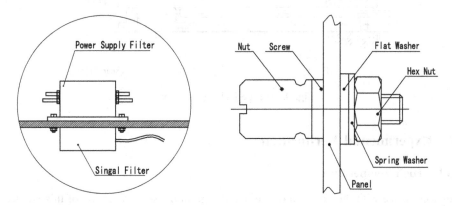

**Fig. 7.** A installation schematic diagram of the filter

**Fig. 8.** The shell-mounted screw combination structure

## 5   Anti-vibration and Anti-impact Design

The hazards caused by the vibration and impact are: the larger resonance is occurred at a certain frequency of excitation; subjected to long-term vibration and shock is easy to make electronic equipment fatigue damage [10]. Vibration shock will increase the mechanical stress of the computer, resulting in poor contact, component deformation and so on.

In order to improve the vibration resistance of the whole machine, the hydraulic shock absorber is installed at the bottom of the reinforcement chassis. The main advantage of this type of shock absorber is that the performance of vibration reduction is good and the installation is convenient.

Panels of the chassis using vacuum brazing technology form a whole, before and after the cover plate are connected to the box through screws, which forms a closed whole to improve the anti-vibration impact capability of the chassis. It takes anti-loose measures to fixing screws, and pan head screws are generally with spring washers and flat washers, and countersunk screws plus thread glue for anti-loose treatment.

The module in the chassis is in the form of plug that the capability of anti-vibration impact is weak. Therefore, the wedge locking mechanism is designed as shown in Fig. 9, which consists of a front slider, a wedge block, a rear slider and a screw. The block contacted with the wedge block is designed as a bevel, which makes the locking structure riveted to the left and right sides of the printed board by rivets. The module is inserted into the groove of the chassis vertically, and the tightening force is applied to the screw clockwise, then the slider will move along the wedge-shaped surface, which contacts with the guide groove surface in the left and right direction to until the lock.

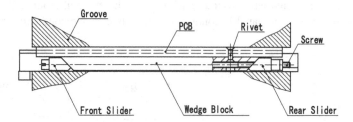

**Fig. 9.** Wedge locking mechanism

## 6  Experimental Verification

### 6.1  High Temperature Test

In accordance with the program of thermal design in the second section of this article, the reinforcement computer completing the assembly and commissioning passes successfully the high and low temperature tests and 120 h reliability assessment in the conditions of 55 °C ambient temperature. Using the Automation Test System ATM2400 and AccuSense UTS1000 thermocouple sensors, the test points are set up in the key components of the main module of the reinforcement chassis. The temperatures of key devices are shown in Table 1.

**Table 1.** Temperature of key devices (Unit: °C)

| Serial number | Test points | Main module 1 | Main module 2 | Main module 3 |
|---|---|---|---|---|
| 1 | CPU | 80.3 | 84 | 82.3 |
| 2 | Video card | 75.4 | 78.8 | 77.2 |
| 3 | North Bridge | 71.5 | 73.4 | 72.6 |

As can be seen from the data in Table 1, the CPU shell temperature in the main module 2 is 84 °C and the CPU shell temperature in the main module 1 is 80.3 °C. As can be seen from shell temperatures, three main modules can work normally and meet thermal design requirements. Therefore, results of the test show that the structure of anti-harsh environment reinforcement is reasonable and can meet the machine's cooling needs.

## 6.2  Vibration Test

In order to verify the adaptability and structural integrity of the reinforcement chassis in the condition of vibration, the vibration test of the reinforcement chassis is carried out strictly in accordance with the requirements of GJB322A-98. The chassis will be librated for 2 h at a frequency of 160 Hz, acceleration 2.5 g, and the chassis is without significant deformation, as well as cracks and shedding phenomenon, and functional indicators are normal, which meets the needs of a variety of harsh environments fully.

# 7  Conclusion

The reinforcement chassis passes not only high and low temperature tests and electromagnetic compatibility test, but also a series of tests such as vibration. The results show that the structure of the chassis, the strength of the design and thermal design are reasonable. The chassis is compact, lightweight, as well as high space utilization, and the functional modules of the cabinet arrange neatly and clearly. On the basis of ensuring the function of the device, its appearance is simple and generous, which gets the user's praise.

# References

1. Kun, L., Lianfa, Y., Weizhi, P., Guohua, F., et al.: Structural design and dynamics simulation for anti-adverse circumstance cabinet. Mech. Des. Manufact. **9**(9), 35–37 (2012)
2. Haijun, Z., Jian, J.: The construction design about a military ruggedized cabinet. In: Proceedings of the Conference on Mechanical and Electrical Engineering for the Year 2005. Electronic Industry Press, Nanjing (2005)
3. Li, Y.: A small cabinet structure and strengthening protection design. Modern Manufacturing Engineering, No. 7, 123–125 (2012)
4. People's Republic of China National Military Standards, GJB/ Z299B-99: The Reliability of Electronic Equipment Design Handbook. The General Armament Department Military Standard Publishing Unit, Beijing, 1 January 1999
5. Chengti, Q., Dunshu, Z., Quanxing, J., et al.: Electronic Device Structure Design Principles. Southeast University Press, Nanjing (2007)
6. Li, H.: Reinforced VXI test chassis development. Harbin Institute of Technology, Harbin (2010)
7. Yan, S.: Electromagnetic shielding design of military portable reinforced computer. Comput. Eng. Appl. **44**(1), 238–239 (2008)
8. Shanshan, W.: Prediction research on shielding effectiveness of electronic equipment box. Harbin University of Science and Technology, Harbin, March 2010
9. Hongmin, L., Zhiyong, Y., Wanyu, L.: Engineering Electromagnetic Compatibility. Xi'an University of Electronic Science and Technology Press, Xi'an (2012)
10. Yingbao, D.: Design on a new type of reinforced computer cabinet. Comput. Netw. **29**(10), 42–44 (2011)

# A High Efficient Control Flow Authentication Method Basing on Loop Isolation

Qingran Wang[1(✉)], Wei Guo[1], Dazhi Sun[1,2], and Jizeng Wei[1]

[1] Tianjin Advanced Network Key Lab, School of Computer Science
and Technology, Tianjin University, Tianjin, China
{qrwang,weiguo,sundazhi,weijizeng}@tju.edu.cn
[2] State Key Laboratory of Information Security,
Institute of Information Engineering, Chinese Academy of Sciences,
Beijing 100093, China

**Abstract.** In spite of numerous protection schemes, embedded systems are still faced with the danger of being attacked, especially at run time. Some 'trusted' programs may be attacked and then result in unintended behaviors, such as jumping to malicious code and leakage of sensitive data. Control flow authentication is one of efficient methods to protect the security of embedded system by ensuring system run along the designed control flow path. In this paper, we propose a new control flow authentication method to further improve the efficiency. A hardware monitor on chip is designed to help authenticate most control flow edges. And the control flow edges in loops are isolated and protected by self-validation software. This software method inserts assembly code upon every basic blocks in a loop to authenticate control flow edges by computing three validation variables. This loop isolation method helps hardware monitor to protect control flow edges which are repeatedly validated in loops to reduce validation times. With this combination, both performance and fault coverage rate have improved compared to traditional methods. To evaluate the performance, we built the system based on ARM v7-A architecture and simulated it using the cycle-accurate simulator GEM5 with SPEC2006 benchmarks.

**Keywords:** Trusted computing · Control flow authentication
Control flow attacks · Computer security

## 1 Introduction

The embedded system protection methods have been developing all the time with the development of embedded technology. In some critical industries, especially the financial industry and aerospace industry, the security and reliability of embedded devices are extremely important. The threat of embedded systems comes from many aspects. In space environment or in an electronic circuit, high energy particles from cosmic rays or an alpha particle can disturb the functionality of embedded devices [1]. Although this transient fault may not cause permanent damage to the chip, it can also affect the reliability of the embedded system. Other threats come from malicious attacks on chips. To steal sensitive data, attackers may modify binaries or program's control flow to link to untrusted library functions or jump to malicious code in static or at run time [2].

© Springer Nature Singapore Pte Ltd. 2018
W. Xu et al. (Eds.): NCCET 2017, CCIS 600, pp. 96–103, 2018.
https://doi.org/10.1007/978-981-10-7844-6_10

If malicious attacks occur before program runs, some traditional security protection methods such as Trusted Platform Module (TPM) could find them by checking the integrity of the binary [3]. This time we should validate programs at run time. But validating program executions at run-time is a difficult work.

Detecting attacks occurring at run time needs to validate the execution of the entire program at run time. General method is combining integrity checking with control flow validation. Checking the integrity of BBs (basic block) can detect attacks which modify instructions or add extra malicious code in BB. Validating control flow paths can detect attacks which let programs jump to malicious code or link to malicious library functions. The most common adopted scheme is using an extra hardware to monitor system, compute signatures and validate the control flow [2, 4, 5, 7]. Some traditional hardware methods, such as run-time execution monitoring (REM) [4] and the hardware-assisted run-time monitor proposed by Arora [5], belong to this kind. Arora extracts every possible control flow edges from assembly source code and stores target addresses into binaries. When program runs, the extra hardware component catches every jump instructions and compares the target addresses with the stored addresses. The system executes this jump instruction only if there is a stored target address that matches the current target address. Due to the introduction of an additional hardware component and the waiting time for comparison results, the performance overhead of this control flow authentication method is high. To accelerate the comparison procedure, Aktas adds a special cache to the system [2]. But the performance is not ideal as well because the modified method still tries to authenticate every control flow edges.

To overcome the shortcomings of hardware-assisted control flow authentication method, pure software-based methods without any extra hardware support are proposed [1, 8, 9]. In Abstract Control Signatures (ACS), Khudia divides a program as several regions and each region has a signature variable [1]. When program runs, the signature variable in a region changes with different BBs and is checked in the end of a region. This software-based authentication method can effectively reduce the number of verification and does not need any extra hardware support. However, due to the reduced authentication mechanism, wrong computing results caused by attacks occurring in a region may have already been written in memory before authentication. The fault coverage of this method is lower compared to the hardware-assisted methods.

In this paper, we propose a high efficient control flow authentication method, which has high fault coverage rate while having low performance overhead. This method uses a special hardware (monitor) to monitor and compare the target addresses of jump instructions. But the control flow edges in loops are protected by a software-based self-validation method. When program runs to a loop, monitor stops authenticating control flow edges and the self-validation software starts to protect the control flow in the loop until program jumps out of this loop. Our special protection for control flow in loops is not only because this method can reduce the authentication times, but also because the control flow in loops is repeatedly validated. The control flow edges in a loop would be validated several times before program jumps out of the loop. If every repeated control flow edges are validated by hardware monitor, a lot of time will be wasted waiting for comparison results. Using the software-based method can effectively reduce the performance overhead.

The remainder of this paper is organized as follows. In Sect. 2, we introduce the designs of the high efficient control flow authentication method from a global perspective. And the hardware part and the software part of this method will be discussed. In Sect. 3, the experiment steps will be introduced and the evaluation results will be analyzed as well. In the end, we will conclude this paper in Sect. 4.

## 2 The High Efficient Control Flow Protection Method

In this section, we describe the proposed control flow protection method in three parts. First, we will introduce the preprocessing stage. In this stage, we prepare correct control flow entries and construct special binaries. Second, we will explain the principle of how does program protect control flow in loops by software-based method. In the end, the hardware part of this method will be introduced.

### 2.1 Preprocessing Stage

The proposed control flow protection method adds a hardware component on chip to authenticate most control flow, but uses a self-validation method to protect control flow in loops. Before system runs, we need to prepare correct control flow entries for hardware validation and add self-validation code to construct a special binary.

Just as Fig. 1 shows, we designs a script to do preprocessing work. First, we analyze the assembly code to find every BBs and find the loops of the program according to the strong connectedness. Then we insert the self-validation code upon BBs in loops. After compiling the modified assembly code, we get the special binary. But we also need the information of the correct control flow edges. So we decompile the binary and get the physical addresses to generate control flow entries and store them into CFG-memory.

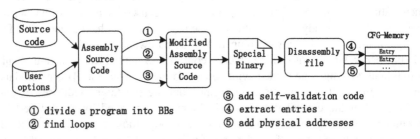

① divide a program into BBs
② find loops
③ add self-validation code
④ extract entries
⑤ add physical addresses

**Fig. 1.** Construct special binaries and prepare correct control flow entries

### 2.2 Protecting Control Flow Edges in Loops

The self-validation code inserted in a special binary can protect control flow in loops without hardware support. In a loop, each BB has three variables which are $W$, $d$ and $D$ for BB weight, weight difference and BB distinction, respectively. The main idea of loop isolation method is using $W$ and $D$ of current BB with $d$ of target BB to compute a temporary BB weight $W_t$ before program jumps to target BB. If $W_t$ equals to target BB's $W$, we think this control flow edge is legal. The path weight of every control flow edges linking two nodes directly is 1. The weight value $W$ of a node is the max value adding all path weights along the longest path from one node to this node. And the $d$ and $D$ of a node is computed using the algorithm shown in Procedure 1.

---

**Procedure 1 Algorithm to compute $d$ and $D$ of a node**
**Control flow from node $V_i$ to node $V_j$**

---

If Pre_node($V_j$) == 1
    $d_j = W_i \oplus W_j; D_j = W_j \oplus W_j;$
Else if Pre_node($V_j$) > 1
    Standard_node($V_j$) = $V_{i1}$
    $d_j = W_{i1} \oplus W_j; D_{i1} = W_{i1} \oplus W_{i1}; D_{i2} = W_{i1} \oplus W_{i2};$

---

After preparing all the three validation variables, we can use them to do authentication work. As Fig. 2 shows, there is an example of how we protect control flow in a loop. After dividing BBs and finding loops, we add self-validation code upon each code in a loop. In the loop of Fig. 2, the path from $V_1$ to $V_2$ is legal, because the computed weight value $W_t = W_1 \oplus d_2 \oplus D_1 = W_1 \oplus W_1 \oplus W_2 \oplus W_1 \oplus W_1$ equals to $W_2$. But the path from $V_1$ to $V_4$ is illegal, because the computed weight value $W_t = W_1 \oplus d_4 \oplus D_1 = W_1 \oplus W_2 \oplus W_4 \oplus W_1 \oplus W_1$ does not equal to $W_4$. And the inserted code upon each BB is shown as the rightmost side of the Fig. 2.

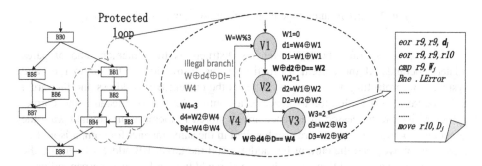

**Fig. 2.** Add self-validation code to protect control flow in loops

## 2.3 Using the Hardware Monitor to Protect Other Control Flow Edges

The proposed control flow protection method has two working modes which are normal mode and protecting mode. When system needs to strictly protect control flow paths, system enters the protecting mode and uses the special hardware component to detect every control flow edges. Otherwise, the system runs in normal mode. We use the debugging instruction 'bkpt' with different operand code to form two special switching instructions ('bkpt 0x01' and 'bkpt 0x02') to switch on or switch off the protecting mode of system.

Next to the processor, there is a special hardware component which called 'Monitor'. The Monitor is placed on chip and can exchange information with the processor. Just as Fig. 3 shows, the Monitor is connected with processor and is consisted of three parts witch are 'Entry Generator', 'Decryptor' and 'Comparator'. The Entry Generator in Monitor is used to pack the source address and the target address of one control flow edge into a formal entry waited to be compared. The Decryptor is used to decrypt the encrypted entry stored in memory and the Comparator is used to compare two entries.

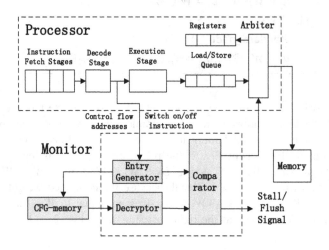

**Fig. 3.** Architecture of the proposed control flow protection method.

When program runs, processor fetches instructions from memory and prepares related operands. If the current instruction is the instruction of the jump type and system is in protecting mode, processor sends the current BB's address and the target BB's address to the Monitor to generate a control flow entry. Because the correct entries which are processed in advance are all stored in memory in a formal way, the generated control flow entries are also handled in the same manner for comparison. In a formal entry, we need the current BB address and the target BB address to ensure the uniqueness of the control flow entry. But we also add two hash values corresponding to two addressed to help accelerate the comparison procedure.

After generating a control flow entry, the Monitor searches the CFG-memory for the matched control flow entry. If there is a match, the controller of the CFG-memory returns the matched entry, or else returns the last searched entry back. Because the correct entries stored in memory is encrypted. The monitor needs to decrypt the entry first and then compares the returned entry with the generated entry to authenticate current control flow edge. If two entries match, the current control flow edge is proved to be legal and system lets the computed results be written to registers or memory, or else the Monitor sends stall signal to system.

## 3  Experiment and Evaluation

In this section, we evaluate the performance overhead of the efficient control flow protection method by comparing this method with a traditional hardware-based method [5]. At the same time, we also inject faults in programs to evaluate the fault coverage rate. The cycle-accurate simulator GEM5 [10] is used to simulate the system implementing the proposed method in SE (system call) mode. All evaluation results are collected through benchmark SPEC2006 in architecture of ARMv7-A. To accelerate the simulation procedure, we use the SimPoint [11] technique. More detailed simulation configurations are shown in Table 1.

**Table 1.** GEM5 simulation parameters.

| Architecture parameter | Configuration |
|---|---|
| Simulation configuration | Out-of-order core |
| Simulation mode | Syscall emulation |
| CPU clock | 2 GHZ |
| Memory size | 7 GB |
| Cache | 32 KB L1 DCache |
| | 32 KB L1 ICache |
| | 128 KB L2 Cache |

For evaluation, we use the IPC (Instructions per Cycle) to measure performance overhead. In Fig. 4, we compare the performance overhead with the hardware-assisted run-time protection method [5] by running the subset of SEPC2006 (bzip2, mcf, soplex, povray, hmmer, sjeng and libquantum). Results show average performance overhead of our method is about 40% while the performance overhead of traditional hardware-assisted method is more than 60% on average. The decrease of about 20% of performance overhead is mainly because that our method does not need to protect the control flow in loops, thus reducing the number of computing and comparison waiting time.

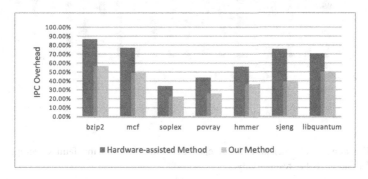

**Fig. 4.** Performance overhead of our method compared with hardware-assisted method.

We also inject faults to the assembly code to evaluate the fault coverage rate of the proposed method. There are five types of faults which are randomly applied to the assembly code:

- Change the jump target (instruction in loop) form BB in loop to another BB in the same loop;
- Change the jump target (instruction in loop) form BB in loop to BB out of loop;
- Change the jump target (instruction is not in loop) out of the loop;
- Change the content of instructions;
- Add or delete several instructions in BB.

After compiling and running the modified binaries on system, faults may be detected or cause damage. The results are classified into four categories:

- WAnswer: Result in wrong answer (fail to detect);
- CTDetect: Detected in compiling stage;
- RDetect: Detected by different control flow protection method;
- SFailure: The injected faults result in simulation termination.

We compare the fault coverage rate of our method with CFCSS and ACS. Figure 5 shows the results of these three methods respectively. We implement three methods in 7 benchmarks. The numbers in the brackets behind each benchmark indicate the current entry correspond to different methods. Of the four types of results mentioned above, only the 'WAnswer' indicates that the fault has not been detected. The results show the fault coverage of our method is about 96% while other two methods are less than 95% and 94% respectively. This may be because our method authenticates every control flow edges in loops, while the ACS only checks the signature variable when program exits the region. And using the hardware component (the Monitor) can also help improve the fault coverage compared with CFCSS.

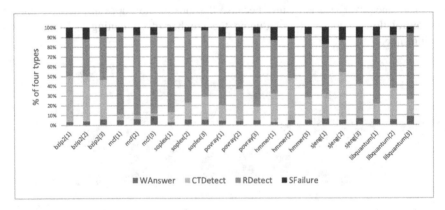

**Fig. 5.** The number (1), (2) and (3) of each benchmark shows the fault coverage of Ours, CFCSS [8] and ACS [1] respectively.

# 4  Conclusions

In this paper, we proposed a high efficient control flow protection method by combining hardware-assisted method with software-based method. The hardware monitor on chip helps system authenticate most control flow edges, while a software method is designed to protect control flow in loops to reduce the unnecessary repetitive comparisons. To achieve this method, we also designed many preprocessing programs.

To evaluate the performance overhead and the fault coverage, we implemented this method on GEM5 simulator through benchmark SPEC2006. The performance overhead is about 40% on average, down by 20% compared to traditional hardware-assisted method. And the fault coverage rate is about 96% which is higher than the pure software-based method ACS and CFCSS.

**Acknowledgements.** The work was supported in part by China Scholarship Council, in part by the Open Project of Shanghai Key Laboratory of Trustworthy Computing under Grant No. 07dz22304201402, and in part by the Natural Science Foundation of Tianjin under Grant No. 11JCZDJC15800.

# References

1. Khudia, D.S., Mahlke, S.: Low cost control flow protection using abstract control signatures. ACM Sigplan Not. **5**(48), 3–12 (2016)
2. Aktas, E., Afram, F., Ghose, K.: Continuous, low overhead, run-time validation of program executions. In: IEEE/ACM International Symposium on Microarchitecture, pp. 229–241. IEEE Computer Society (2014)
3. Trusted Platform Module spec, http://www.trustedcomputinggroup.org/
4. Fiskiran, A.M., Lee, R.B.: Runtime execution monitoring (REM) to detect and prevent malicious code execution, pp. 452–457. IEEE Computer Society (2004)
5. Arora, D., et al.: Hardware-assisted run-time monitoring for secure program execution on embedded processors. IEEE Trans. Very Large Scale Integr. Syst. **14**, 1295–1308 (2006). IEEE
6. Davi, L., Koeberl, P., Sadeghi, A.R.: Hardware-assisted fine-grained control-flow integrity: towards efficient protection of embedded systems against software exploitation. In: Design Automation Conference, pp. 1–6. IEEE (2014)
7. Clercq, R.D., et al.: SOFIA: software and control flow integrity architecture. In: Design, Automation & Test in Europe Conference & Exhibition, pp. 1172–1177. Elsevier (2016)
8. Oh, N., Shirvani, P.P., Mccluskey, E.J.: Control-flow checking by software signatures. IEEE Trans. Reliab. **51**, 111–122 (2002). IEEE
9. Das, S., Zhang, W., Liu, Y.: A fine-grained control flow integrity approach against runtime memory attacks for embedded systems. IEEE Trans. Very Large Scale Integr. Syst., 1–15 (2016). IEEE
10. Binkert, N., Beckmann, B., Black, G., et al.: The gem5 simulator. ACM SIGARCH Comput. Archit. News **2**(39), 1–7 (2011)
11. Ganesan, K., Panwar, D., John, L.K.: Generation, validation and analysis of SPEC CPU2006 simulation points based on branch, memory and TLB characteristics. In: Computer Performance Evaluation and Benchmarking, SPEC Benchmark Workshop, pp. 121–137. ACM, Austin (2009)

# Malware Detection with Convolutional Neural Network Using Hardware Events

Wei Guo, Tenghai Wang[(⊠)], and Jizeng Wei

Tianjin Advanced Network Key Lab, School of Computer Science
and Technology, Tianjin University, Tianjin, China
{weiguo,tenghaiwang,weijizeng}@tju.edu.cn

**Abstract.** Detection of malicious programs (i.e., malwares) is a great challenge due to increasing amount and variety of attacks. Recent works have shown that machine learning, especially neural network, performs well in malware detection. In this paper, convolution neural network (CNN) is used to build the malware classification model. Different from other works, our work uses hardware events to generate the feature image of programs. These hardware events, such as cache miss rate, branch misprediction rate, can be collected from the performance counter in the Intel CPUs. We train CNN with kinds of data sizes and kernel sizes, and evaluate the result by the area under a receiver operating characteristics (ROC) curve (AUC). The results show the proposed classification model can achieve AUC = 0.9973 in best case and the influence by the data size or kernel size is very little. Moreover, by comparison with other CNNs trained with software-based features, it is indicated that the proposed model has higher accuracy than the other ones.

**Keywords:** Malware detection · Hardware events
Convolution neural network

## 1 Introduction

Malware, known as one of the great threats to computers, disrupts computer files and steals private information. It's shown on AV TEST that more than 390,000 new malicious programs are registered every day in 2017 [1]. On the other hand, malware detection is becoming more difficult because of its huge quantity and random variants.

To keep computer systems from malware's threat, numerous methods for malware detection have been put forward. Especially in recent years, many researchers have made significant progress on using machine learning to help with resisting malware. For example, it was verified that execution traces, system calls, control flow and et al. can be trained with various machine learning algorithms to reveal malware [2–4]. Nevertheless, these software features can be covered by deliberate attackers.

CNN is well known for its excellent ability in the field of image recognition. However, Tobiyama et al. [5] have showed that CNN can also perform well in malware detection. They logged API calls and program behavior, trained RNN (Recurrent Neural Network) with these log files to generate feature images, and then trained CNN with the generated feature images. Although it's an important accomplishment, as

W. Xu et al. (Eds.): NCCET 2017, CCIS 600, pp. 104–115, 2018.
https://doi.org/10.1007/978-981-10-7844-6_11

mentioned above, using software-based features is just another potential vulnerability that an attacker can exploit.

To avoid this leak, hardware-based features are considered in this paper. Based on Intel processor, VTune tools [6] was used to sample hardware events and the malware and benign programs were classified by trained CNN. The main contributions of this paper are as follows:

1. This paper proposes a new dynamic malware detection method, training CNN with hardware-based features to build the classification model.
2. This paper evaluates the proposed method and proves its high accuracy rate and low error rate both for malicious and benign programs.
3. The results demonstrate that both the data size and the kernel size have little influence on our classification model.

The rest of the paper is organized as follows. The previous malware detection methods are introduced in Sect. 2. Then in Sect. 3, we introduce the details of the proposed hardware event based CNN model for malwares detection. The experimental setup, including dataset, environment and network parameters, is presented in Sect. 4. The experimental evaluation is shown in Sect. 5, and we give a conclusion in Sect. 6.

## 2  Related Works

Malware detection methods can be classified into two types by the time when malware is detecting. The one is static detection, which means detect malware before its execution, and the other one is dynamic detection, which means detect malware when it's running.

The main idea of static detection is to create a malware database which is consisted of signatures of malware and then check one's signature in the database before a program executes. Cesare and Xiang [7] proposed a novel algorithm for constructing a control flow graph signature using the decompilation technique of structuring in 2010. They used a structuring algorithm to recover high level structured control flow from a normal control flow graph. The structured control flow formed the signature database, and malware is detected by calculating the similarity ratio. Cesare and Xiang [8] proposed another way to build the database in 2011. They used a polynomial time algorithm to generate q-gram features of decompiled control flow graphs to construct feature vectors, and then defined a distance metric to decide whether a program is malicious.

Since the database is always slow to update, the static detection is hard to defend zero-day exploits. The other type, dynamic detection, is getting increasingly attention. Wu and Hung [9] and Yeh et al. [10] extracted 25 API calls and 13 types of activities from Android applications and then extended them to high dimensions as features for the input of SVM (support vector machine) or CNN. They demonstrated that CNN achieved better accuracy and FPR (false positive rate) than SVM, but both with a high FNR (false negative rate). Das et al. [11] innovatively used a frequency-centralized model for feature construction and designed an architecture of the detection tool which named GuardOL in FPGA. As malware can be divided into many types, like viruses, worms, trojans and so on, Khasawneh et al. [12] used ensemble learning to improve the performance of the hardware detectors. They first built specialized detectors which were trained only with malware that matches the detector type and general detectors which were trained with mixed types of malware. Then they proved that specialized detectors outperform general detectors. Finally, they combinate specialized detectors and general detectors in different ways to improve the detectors' performance.

Besides building classifier using machine learning, determining a baseline or a threshold for programs can also help distinguishing malware. Tang et al. [13] built classification models to describe the baseline characteristics for programs. They selected some architectural events and microarchitectural events as features, and trained them with unsupervised one-class machine learning techniques to model characteristics. After Training and calculating thresholds, Kompalli [14] found that any process generating BPU (Branch Prediction Unit) value over 34% can be determined as malware.

## 3   Hardware Event Based CNN Model for Malwares Detection

As mentioned in previous sections, static detection is always sluggish in new malware detecting, and detectors based on software features can be hoodwinked by deliberate attackers who may use novel coding style. Considering these, we design a dynamic detection method and used hardware events as features.

The overview of proposed method is shown in Fig. 1. Hardware events are used to describe the feature of programs. The occurrence times of each event are countered by performance counter when the program is running. This is similar to the construction of gray scale images. To each event corresponds a pixel, and to the number of times it occurs corresponds the gray value. For that reason, we presume that CNN can be used to create the classifier. As shown in Fig. 1, after converting the collected hardware event data to images, the CNN trains these images to build a classifier.

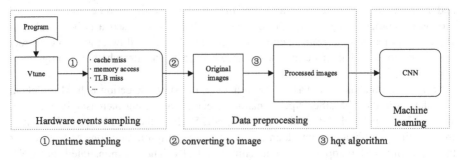

**Fig. 1.** Overview of proposed method

### 3.1   Hardware Events

There are many hardware events happening as a program running, such as cache misses rate, branch mispredictions rate, memory accesses times and so on. Attacks usually bring with enormous shift of hardware events. For example, spyware, a type of malware which collects personal information, causes the increase of memory accesses. In our work, VTune is used to sample these hardware events by the Performance monitoring unit (PMU) [15] in Intel CPUs. PMU was first introduced in the Pentium CPU and today all Intel mainstream series CPUs, such as i3, i5 and i7, are equipped with it. It means that the proposed method can be widely applied to any machine with Intel CPUs regardless of the operation system.

There are more than 200 entries of hardware events can be collected by VTune, but some of them only happen in rare programs and some others always happen little times in both malware and benign programs. Finally, for the fair comparison we chose 184 entries of hardware events which can always be collected with proper values, and some of them are shown in Table 1.

**Table 1.**  Some of selected hardware events

| Event number | Event description |
| --- | --- |
| Event1[a] | Cycles when divide unit is busy executing divide or square root operations. Accounts for integer and floating-point operations |
| Event2[b] | All mispredicted macro branch instructions retired |
| Event3[c] | Core crystal clock cycles when this thread is unhalted and the other thread is halted |
| Event4[d] | Counts when there is a transition from ring 1, 2 or 3 to ring 0 |
| Event5[e] | Load misses in all DTLB levels that cause page walks |
| Event6[f] | Cycles total of 1 uop is executed on all ports and Reservation Station was not empty |
| Event7[g] | Retired instructions who experienced iTLB true miss |
| Event8[h] | Retired instructions who experienced Instruction L1 Cache true miss |
| Event9[i] | Cycles when uops are being delivered to Instruction Decode Queue from Decode Stream Buffer path |
| Event10[j] | Requests from the L1/L2/L3 hardware prefetchers or load software prefetches that hit L2 cache |

[a] Event1 is ARITH.DIVIDER_ACTIVE
[b] Event2 is BR_MISP_RETIRED.ALL_BRANCHES
[c] Event3 is CPU_CLK_THREAD_UNHALTED.ONE_THREAD_ACTIVE
[d] Event4 is CPU_CLK_UNHALTED.RING0_TRANS
[e] Event5 is DTLB_LOAD_MISSES.MISS_CAUSES_A_WALK
[f] Event6 is EXE_ACTIVITY.1_PORTS_UTIL
[g] Event7 is FRONTED_RETIRED.ITLB_MISS
[h] Event8 is FRONTED_RETIRED.L1I_MISS
[i] Event9 is IDQ.DSB_CYCLES
[j] Event10 is L2_RQSTS.PF_HIT

Hardware events in Table 1 are related to different event types. There are still many other types, and for every type, there are more detailed events. For example, some events are related to Store Buffer, like EXE_ACTIVITY.BOUND_ON_STORES, which represent cycles where the Store Buffer was full and no outstanding load. Another example is the type of branch misprediction. Except Event2 in Table 1, other events related to branch misprediction are BR_MISP_RETIRED.CONDITIONAL (mispredicted conditional branch instructions retired), BR_MISP_RETIRED.NEAR_-TAKEN (Number of near branch instructions retired that were mispredicted and taken), BR_MISP_RETIRED.NEAR_CALL (mispredicted direct and indirect near call instructions retired), etc. To summarize, we sampled almost all the hardware events that could happen during a program's running, to make sure that these events can describe a program's behavior completely. For getting more precise data, we run each program multiple times and unified all the data to the same unit (clocktick).

## 3.2    Data Preprocessing

CNN is a neural network designed for image recognition, and it has two special layers named convolution layer and pooling layer. The structure of CNN is shown in Fig. 2.

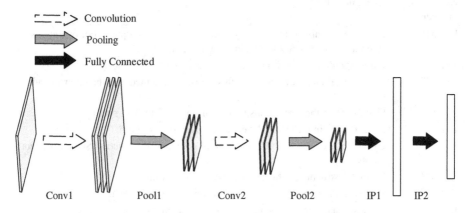

**Fig. 2.**  Structure of CNN

In the convolution layer, a matrix called convolution kernel will be convoluted with a two-dimensional image. The convolution can be defined as Eq. 1,

$$X_i^l = \sigma(X_i^{l-1} * K_i^l + b^l) \tag{1}$$

where
$X_i^l$    gives the output of feature map for location i in convolution layer l;
$\sigma$    is the activation function (e.g., Sigmoid or ReLU);
$X_i^{l-1}$    represents the output of layer l-1 at location i;
$K_i^l$    is the convolution kernel for location i on layer l;
$b^l$    denotes the bias parameter fog layer l.

It's clearly that the convolution is an operation between two matrixes. However, the data we collected is one-dimensional, so it's necessary to transform the data to two-dimensional.

The pooling layer serves to reduce the spatial size of the input feature maps in order to decrease the effect of shifting and control overfitting. Max pooling is used in this work, which chooses the max value of neighbourhoods to form the new matrix.

To make it presentable as input, the data is first reshaped into four different sizes of matrixes, as shown in Table 2. Then we map each element of the matrix to the [0,1] space and multiply 255 to form 256 level gray scale image.

**Table 2.** Sizes of the data

| Item | Size 1 | Size 2 | Size 3 | Size 4 |
|---|---|---|---|---|
| Length | 8 | 23 | 4 | 46 |
| Width | 23 | 8 | 46 | 4 |

These sizes are too small for an image, hence hqx [16] algorithm is considered. Hqx, where "hq" stands for "high quality" and "x" stands for magnification, is one of the pixel art scaling algorithms in image processing. There are three hqx filters: hq2x, hq3x, and hq4x, which magnify by factor of 2, 3, and 4 respectively. Hq4x was used in this work.

The first step of hqx is an analysis of the 3*3 area of the source pixel. The color difference between the central pixel and its 8 nearest neighbors is calculated and then compared to a predefined threshold. After comparison, these pixels are divided into two categories: "close" and "distant" colored. There are 8 neighbors, so it will get 256 possible combinations. The next step is filtering. A lookup table with 256 entries is used, where each entry corresponds to a combination of close/distant colored neighbors, describing how to mix the colors of the source pixel from 3*3 area to get interpolated pixels of the filtered image. For hq4x, one single pixel is expanded to 4*4 block of pixels.

We show two images converted from Size 1 in Fig. 3. Figure 3(a) is an image of malware and Fig. 3(b) is an image of benign program. The circles give three markedly different areas between the two images.

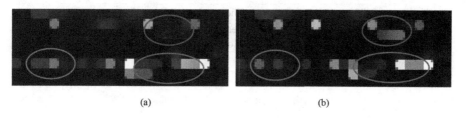

(a)                                                                 (b)

**Fig. 3.** Images converted from Size 1

## 4  Experimental Setup

### 4.1  Dataset and Environment

In our work, we used 200 malicious programs and 100 benign programs as the training data, and 100 malicious programs and 80 benign programs were used as the test data. The malicious programs were download from the VirusShare website [17]. To collect benign programs, we used several benchmarks, such as SPEC2006, MiBench [18], MediaBench [19] and so on.

We apply Vtune tools to a personal computer, installed with 64-bit Ubuntu 14.04 operating system and running an intel Core i7-6700 CPU(3.40 GHz) with 16 GB memory. Both the malicious and benign programs were run under root privilege, ensuring all the functions of these programs can be execute freely.

### 4.2  Network Parameters

As shown in Fig. 2, our CNN has two convolution layers, two pooling layers and two inner product layers. To compare the performance of the classifier in different parameters and find the best network, we tried different kernel size for each size of input. The parameters we used are shown in Table 3.

**Table 3.** Parameters of the CNN

| Item | | Size 1 | Size 2 | Size 3 | Size 4 |
|---|---|---|---|---|---|
| Conv1 | Kernel size | 2/3/4/5 | | 2 | |
| | Other parameters | The number of filters: 20 stride: 1 | | | |
| Pool1 | Kernel size | 2 | | | |
| | Other parameters | The pooling method: MAX stride: 2 | | | |
| Conv2 | Kernel size | 2 | | | |
| | Other parameters | The number of filters: 50 Stride: 1 | | | |
| Pool2 | Kernel size | 2 | | | |
| | Other parameters | The pooling method: MAX stride: 2 | | | |
| IP1[a] | | The number of filters: 500 | | | |
| IP2 | | The number of filters: 2 | | | |
| Solver | | Learning rate: 0.0001 Model: CPU only | | | |

[a] IP is inner product layer

We set our CNN parameters by referring the LeNet [20], which is the typical network used for recognizing hand written digit from images. To analyze the effect of kernel size, we set four kernel sizes, from 2 to 5, in the Conv1 for Size 1 and Size 2. As for Size 3 and Size 4, the kernel size of Conv1 was only set to 2 for analyzing the effect of data size. We will show and compare the results of different parameters in next section.

## 5  Experimental Results and Evaluation

### 5.1  Evaluation Method

A ROC graph is a technique for visualizing, organizing and selecting classifiers based on their performance [21]. The ROC curve is usually used for binary-class classifiers, and it depicts the relationship between true positive rate (TPR) and false positive rate (FPR). In our work, as we are aimed at malware detection, we considered malware as the positive class, and we defined TPR and FPR as Table 4.

**Table 4.** The definition of TPR and FPR

| Input class | Output class | | Formula |
|---|---|---|---|
| | Malware | Benign | |
| Malware | TP | FN | TPR = TP/(TP + FN) |
| Benign | FP | TN | FPR = FP/(FP + TN) |

There are three special points in a ROC curve graph. The lower left point (0,0) represents the classifier never judge a program as malware. By contrast, the upper right point (1,1) represents the classifier treat all programs as malware. The upper left point (0,1) represents a perfect classifier. Stated thus, the classifier is better if the curve is closer to the upper left corner. Naturally, we use Area under an ROC curve (AUC) to evaluate the performance of our model.

### 5.2  Effect of Data Size

We first trained CNN with four different data sizes shown in Table 2, setting the kernel size to 2. Figure 4 shows ROC curves. The AUC of Size 1, 2, 3, 4 were 0.9969, 0.9973, 0.9950, 0.9954 respectively. The difference is very small among these conditions. Therefore, we believe that the data size does not make an influence on the classification model.

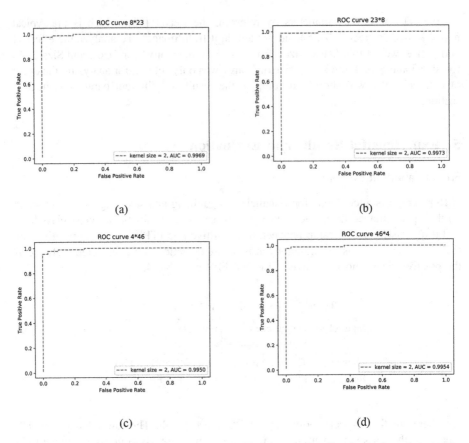

**Fig. 4.** ROC curves of different data sizes. (a) to (d) correspond to Size 1 to 4, kernel sizes = 2.

## 5.3   Effect of Kernel Size

For Size 1 and 2, the CNN was trained with setting the kernel size from 2 to 5. Figure 5 shows the ROC curves of each condition. When the kernel size changed from 3 to 5, the AUC of Size 1were 0.9874, 0.9900, 0.9908 respectively, and for Size 2, the AUC were 0.9958, 09851, 0.9962. The differences are negligible. Hence, we summarized that the kernel size does not affect the classification model.

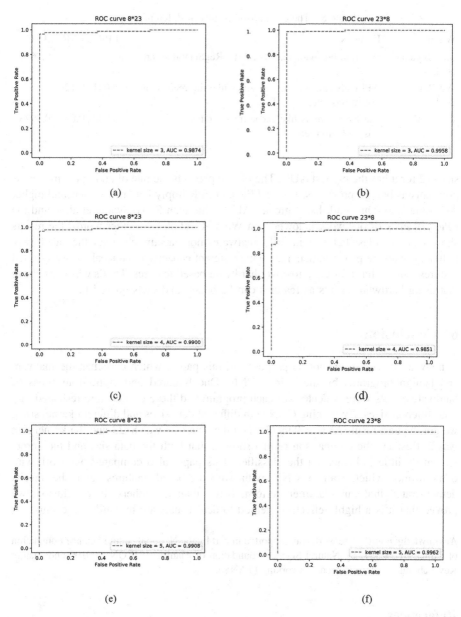

**Fig. 5.** ROC curve of different kernel size. Data size of (a), (c) and (e) is Size 1, and the others is Size 2.

## 5.4    Performance Comparison

As mentioned earlier, Tobiyama et al. [5] and Wu and Hung [9] have trained CNN with software-based features for malware detection. We compared our work with theirs and show the results in Table 5. In our work, we used the result of Size 2 when the kernel

**Table 5.** The comparison results of different works

| Works | Features | FPR | FNR | AUC |
|---|---|---|---|---|
| S. Tobiyama et al. | Program behavior like ReadFile, RegSetValue, etc. | – | – | 0.96 |
| Wu W.C. et al. | API calls and runtime activities like file read, write operations, etc. | 0.041 | 0.129 | – |
| Our work | Hardware events like cache miss, branch misprediction, etc. | 0.033 | 0.034 | 0.9973 |

size is 2 for it has the highest AUC. The FNR represents the rate of taking the malicious programs as benign programs. Lower FPR and FPR imply better classifier, and higher AUC does too. Our work has a greater AUC value than S. Tobiyama et al.'s, and the FPR and FNR of our work is lower than Wu W.C. et al.'s. In other words, the results show that our classifier can identify malware more accurately than the other two. Different malware programmers may have different capacity to conceal software-based features, but it's hard for them to cover hardware-based features. That's why we believe that using hardware events as features can be better, and facts proved it.

## 6  Conclusion

A malware detection method is proposed in this paper, which classifies the malware and benign programs by the trained CNN. One hundred and eighty-four types of hardware events were collected for each program and these events were reshaped into four different sizes. By training CNN with different data sizes and different kernel sizes, we got the best result AUC = 0.9973 when the data size was 8*23 and the kernel size was 2. Besides, the comparison results showed that both the data size and the kernel size made little influence on the classifier. This paper also compared our work with other works which trained CNN with software-based features, and the results demonstrated that our classifier perform better than the others. In conclusion, we proved that it is a highly effective method to detect malware by hardware events.

**Acknowledgement.** The work was supported in part by the National Nature Science Foundation of China, 61402321, by Natural Science Foundation of Tianjin, 15JCQNJC00100 and Tianjin Key Laboratory of Advanced Networking (TANK).

## References

1. The AV-TEST Institute. http://www.av-test.org/en/statistics/malware/. Accessed 25 June 2017
2. Christodorescu, M., Jha, S., Kruegel, C.: Mining specifications of malicious behavior. In: Proceedings of the 1st India Software Engineering Conference, pp. 5–14. ACM (2008)

3. Das, S., Xiao, H., Liu, Y., et al.: Online malware defense using attack behavior model. In: 2016 IEEE International Symposium on Circuits and Systems (ISCAS), pp. 1322–1325. IEEE (2016)
4. Kapoor, A., Dhavale, S.: Control flow graph based multiclass malware detection using bi-normal separation. Def. Sci. J. **66**(2), 138–145 (2016)
5. Tobiyama, S., Yamaguchi, Y., Shimada, H., et al.: Malware detection with deep neural network using process behavior. In: Computer Software and Applications Conference (COMPSAC), vol. 2, pp. 577–582. IEEE (2016)
6. Intel VTune Amplifier 2016. https://software.intel.com/en-us/intel-vtune-amplifier-xe. Accessed 25 June 2017
7. Cesare, S., Xiang, Y.: Classification of malware using structured control flow. In: Eighth Australasian Symposium on Parallel and Distributed Computing, pp. 61–70. Australian Computer Society, Inc. (2010)
8. Cesare, S., Xiang, Y.: Malware variant detection using similarity search over sets of control flow graphs. In: IEEE International Conference on Trust, Security and Privacy in Computing and Communications, vol. 21, pp. 181–189. IEEE (2011)
9. Wu, W.C., Hung, S.H.: DroidDolphin: a dynamic Android malware detection framework using big data and machine learning. In: Proceedings of the 2014 Conference on Research in Adaptive and Convergent Systems. pp. 247–252. ACM (2014)
10. Yeh, C.W., Yeh, W.T., Hung, S.H., et al.: Flattened data in convolutional neural networks: using malware detection as case study. In: Proceedings of the International Conference on Research in Adaptive and Convergent Systems. pp. 130–135. ACM (2016)
11. Das, S., Liu, Y., Zhang, W., et al.: Semantics-based online malware detection: towards efficient real-time protection against malware. IEEE Trans. Inf. Forensics Secur. **11**(2), 289–302 (2016)
12. Khasawneh, K.N., Ozsoy, M., Donovick, C., Abu-Ghazaleh, N., Ponomarev, D.: Ensemble learning for low-level hardware-supported malware detection. In: Bos, H., Monrose, F., Blanc, G. (eds.) RAID 2015. LNCS, vol. 9404, pp. 3–25. Springer, Cham (2015). https://doi.org/10.1007/978-3-319-26362-5_1
13. Tang, A., Sethumadhavan, S., Stolfo, Salvatore J.: Unsupervised anomaly-based malware detection using hardware features. In: Stavrou, A., Bos, H., Portokalidis, G. (eds.) RAID 2014. LNCS, vol. 8688, pp. 109–129. Springer, Cham (2014). https://doi.org/10.1007/978-3-319-11379-1_6
14. Kompalli, S.: Using existing hardware services for malware detection. In: Security and Privacy Workshops (SPW), pp. 204–208. IEEE (2014)
15. Guide, P.: Intel 64 and IA-32 Architectures Software Developers Manual. Volume 3B: System programming Guide, Part 2. Chaps. 18, 19 (2011)
16. Hqx, https://code.google.com/archive/p/hqx/. Accessed 25 June 2017
17. VirusShare. https://virusshare.com/. Accessed 25 June 2017
18. MiBench Version 1.0. http://vhosts.eecs.umich.edu/mibench//. Accessed 25 June 2017
19. MediaBench Consortium. http://mathstat.slu.edu/~fritts/mediabench/. Accessed 25 June 2017
20. Training LeNet on MNIST with Caffe. http://caffe.berkeleyvision.org/gathered/examples/mnist.html. Accessed 25 June 2017
21. Fawcett, T.: An introduction to ROC analysis. Pattern Recogn. Lett. **27**(8), 861–874 (2016)

# Research of Configurable Hybrid Memory Architecture for Big Data Processing

Hongwei Zhou[✉], Rangyu Deng, Quanyou Feng, Xiaoqiang Ni,
and Qiang Dou

College of Computer, National University of Defense Technology,
Changsha 410073, China
forrestzhw@sohu.com

**Abstract.** A configurable hybrid memory architecture (CHMA) for big data processing is proposed in this paper. It includes computing nodes and memory nodes. The computing node can be configured according to the requirement of different applications to improve the applicability of the computing system. The memory node contains the memory control chip and memory network that support to build memory system with different type of memory devices. Each memory control chip contains two memory controllers. Two key technologies are proposed to optimize the bandwidth and latency of memory access for CHMA, one is the multi-channel parallel bus structure, and the other is the cache or buffer structure inserted in memory control chip. Experimental results show that: first, two memory controller are integrated in the memory control chip can maximize the bandwidth efficiency of the memory network; second, the bandwidth of multi-channel parallel bus is balanced with the bandwidth of two memory channels; third, when the cache or buffer structure is inserted in memory control chip, the latency of memory access is reduced and the bandwidth of memory access is improved, the memory access bandwidth of 64-thread stream OpenMP program is increased by 16.86% and the execution speed of NPB-MPI scientific computing applications are improved by an average of 6%.

**Keywords:** Big data · Configurable · Hybrid memory

## 1 Introduction

For the computing system aimed for large data applications, the following characteristics should be available: first, for massive data processing, not only high computing performance but also high throughput and low latency are needed; second, for massive data memory, not only fast access speed is required, but also the reliability and consistency should be kept.

The research is supported by the National Science Foundation of China (61303069, 61602498, 61402502, 61472432).

W. Xu et al. (Eds.): NCCET 2017, CCIS 600, pp. 116–132, 2018.
https://doi.org/10.1007/978-981-10-7844-6_12

In traditional data center or high performance computer, the Cache-DRAM-Disk memory hierarchy and the organization mode of computing nodes and disk array nodes have been unable to meet the memory bandwidth and latency requirements for massive data processing. It restricts the overall performance more obviously, and mainly represents in following four aspects.

- The SRAM in processor meets problems of integrated density, static leakage power and reliability. The SRAM is usually used to Cache in multi-core processor chip. Although it is fast and can match the speed of processor access, it faces some problems during the capacity expansion with the increase of the number of cores in processor chip. Due to the lower integration density, the SRAM will occupy a lot of on-chip area, crowding out the computing resources on chip. At the same time the static energy consumption will increase linearly with the area of on-chip SRAM increasing, and it has become a major source of processor power. In addition, the SRAM unit is easily affected by radiation, resulting in a higher rate of soft error.
- The main memory constructed by DRAM suffers obstacles of power consumption, efficiency, access latency and reliability. The charge leakage, regular refresh, and the entire row of DRAM memory cell being turned on although only partial data needed to be read for each access, these become the important sources of DRAM energy consumption. Research shows that the energy consumption of DRAM memory accounts for about 27%–40% of the whole energy consumption of data centers [1]. Restricted by DRAM's structure, the latency of the DRAM has not been improved obviously with the development of technologies. Although some technologies proposed can improve the access speed in a certain extent, the chip area overhead is increased more obviously, so these technologies haven't become the mainstream [2].
- The development of memory architecture in computer system is confronted with great challenge of reliability. A massively parallel computing system has a large number of DRAM memories, and the Exascale system will fail every two hours. The Cache-DRAM-Disk memory hierarchy need improve reliability by traditional data backup, it will influence computing efficiency greatly due to extra data transfer.
- The memory efficiency cannot be increased linearly with the increase of memory capacity. The memory hierarchy cannot adapt to the requirements of different applications. The dynamic allocation mechanism of memory resources according to different applications needs to be improved.

So, traditional memory architecture is more and more difficult to meet the requirements of the development of big data processing. In order to meet the needs of large data applications, the optimization and transformation of memory architecture is crucial.

There are two ways to improve memory architecture for big data processing: one is to further explore new memory devices, improve memory integration density, reduce power consumption and improve reliability; the other is to combine with the development of new memory devices, improve the memory architecture for data center and high performance computing system. For the first aspect, both the industrial and academic fields have made active research and put forward a series of research results, some of them have been practical. IBM integrates 32 MB embedded DRAM (eDRAM) devices in POWER7 [3]. The magnetic RAM (MRAM) [4, 5], phase change RAM [6, 7] (PCRAM) and a RAM based on the electrical and thermal effect of a metal and metal-oxide layer structure (RRAM) [8, 9] are typical representative of the emerging non-volatile memory (eNVM) and they are developed rapidly. For the second aspect, the research has two directions.

- One direction is combining with the new memory devices and the processor memory hierarchy design to alleviate the memory bottleneck. The related research is the following. The paper [10, 11] discussed the life and energy efficiency problems when PCRAM is used to construct the main memory, and predicts the future of PCRAM and the main memory system based on it. The paper [12, 13] proposed the ways of using eNVM instead of eDRAM to construct on-chip Cache. The paper [14, 15] suggests to construct a register file, Cache and main memory using different types of memory devices. The paper [16–18] discussed the application of eNVM in high performance file system and storage device and architecture level optimization technique oriented eNVM. The Paper [19] studied how the operating system support the eNVM and DRAM mixed memory system.
- The other direction is to change traditional data processing methods. The most typical idea is memory computing in which CPU reads data and calculates directly from memory instead of hard disk. The HANA hardware platform proposed by SAP meets the needs of processing data in memory by expanding the memory capacity of every node [20]. It can perform the required query operations by loading data into memory and continually scanning the entire data table rapidly. Exalytics system proposed by Oracle uses Infiniband network for system interconnection to achieve high-speed data processing and analysis for mass data processing [21]. The RAMCloud proposed by Stanford University connects multiple servers through high-speed data center network to provide Key-Value storage based on memory in which data scattered in all server memory and can realize 100–1000 TB memory capacity [22]. The above three kinds of memory solutions are all based on the traditional DRAM memory, and the memory data need to be backed up to the hard disk and another nonvolatile memory device. The data backup will reduce the efficiency of memory computing significantly.

In summary, memory computing for large data processing has more requirements and challenges to future memory architecture. With the increase of data scale, the main memory system based on DRAM is becoming more and more difficult to satisfy the development of memory computing technology. Due to the low power and nonvolatile features, the time of implementing on-chip memory architectures using NVM, partially or entirely, instead of SRAM, is ripe. This paper presents configurable hybrid memory architecture (CHMA) for large data processing to alleviate the performance bottleneck of current memory system based on DRAM.

## 2 Configurable Hybrid Memory Architecture

The overall architecture of the configurable hybrid memory architecture for large data processing is shown in Fig. 1. The CHMA includes computing nodes and memory nodes. The computing nodes provide computing resource for computing system of big data processing, and can be configured according to different needs of computing ability for different application to improve the applicability of the calculation system. The computing resource of computing nodes includes multiple cores on processor chip, the on-chip caches tightly coupled with the processor cores, and local memories that contain different types of memory devices. As shown in Fig. 1, local memory can be constructed by mixed memory using DDR and NVM devices at the same time.

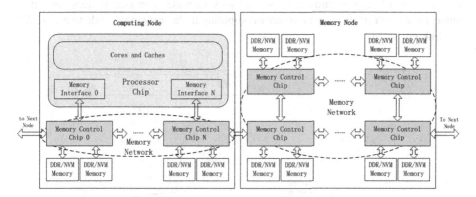

**Fig. 1.** Structure diagram of the configurable hybrid memory architecture

The cores and caches in computing node are connected with multiple memory control chips through multiple memory interfaces. They can access memory system concurrently to meet the requirements of memory bandwidth. Each memory control chip includes a plurality of interconnect ports. One port is connected with the memory interface, two ports are connected with DDR/NVM local memory separately, and other else ports are used to connect memory control chip in adjacent computing node or memory node. Memory control chip has the function of network router and can be used to build memory network with various topological structure. In addition to sending the memory request from processor chip to the memory system within the local computing node, the memory request can be send to memory system in other remote nodes through the memory network. Memory node contain multiple memory control chips connected by memory network and no cores and caches exist. Memory node support different types of memory device to form hybrid memory system. In CHMA, if the capacity of local memory is insufficient during an application is running, this application can send a memory allocation request to other memory control chip in adjacent memory node without interrupting the normal operation. The memory node which receives the memory allocation request will allocates some memory space to the request node according to certain scheduling and allocation strategies and its memory usage status. For the applications issuing the request, the remote memory space allo-cated can be used as local memory to alleviate the memory capacity shortage.

## 2.1 The Design and Configuration of Computing Node

Figure 2 is a schematic diagram of a computing node. As shown, a computing node contains a processor chip and many memory control chips. The processor chip contains multiple memory interfaces. The memory control chip contains a router and two DDR/NVM memory controllers. The processor chip and the memory control chip are communicated each other through a high-speed memory link. A memory link master locates in processor chip and a memory link slave locates in memory control chip. The router in memory control chip has interconnect ports to interconnect with adjacent memory control chip to build memory network in node. The side routers can inter-connect with the routers located in other computing node or memory node to realize the interlink on board.

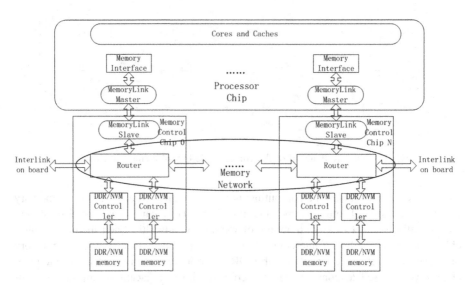

**Fig. 2.** Schematic diagram of computing node

Computing nodes provide the computing ability for computing system of big data processing. Taking into account the different requirements of memory bandwidth and access latency for different applications, computer node can be configured by different schemes to improve the applicability. For the applications that need high memory bandwidth and low latency, the recommended configuration of computing node is shown in the left picture of Fig. 3. As the picture shown, the processor chip contains multiple processor clusters (each cluster contains multiple processor cores sharing cache). Multiple processor clusters are interconnected each other through the network on chip (NoC) to construct a tightly coupled multiprocessor architecture. The memory access requests are sent to different memory interface by NoC according to the address space partition. The total memory access bandwidth is increased by parallel memory access. The dedicated NoC facilitates data sharing between clusters and improves the speed of remote data access. If the application has less requirement for memory bandwidth and latency, the computing node is recommended to be configured as shown in the right picture of Fig. 3. In this mode, each cluster has independent memory access interface, and no dedicated NoC is used. Data sharing and migration depends on memory network absolutely. The disadvantage of this mode is the latency of memory network is larger than the dedicated NoC network.

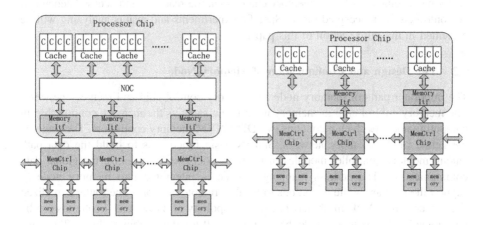

**Fig. 3.** Design and configuration of computing node

Compared with the traditional multi-core processor architecture, placing the memory controller in the independent memory control chip has both advantages and disadvantages. The advantages are as the following.

- The design of the processor chip can be simplified. For the processor has more cores, due to most resource of chip is used to implement the cores and caches, the demand on the memory bandwidth has been increased obviously. If more memory access channels are integrated into processor chip, it will further increase the area of the chip, and also increase the number of chip pins, causing great difficulties to package design and board layout. The memory control chips are placed outside of the processor chip, not only can simplify the design of processor chip, reduce area and power consumption of the chip, but also can increase the margin of distant between two chips, bring the convenient for PCB design.
- The independent memory control chip can improve the design flexibility of memory system. The memory control chips can be connected with processor chip through high-speed and high-bandwidth bus, improving memory bandwidth and scalability of system. The memory control chips can be interconnected each other by memory network to provide the ability of data transfer between two memory control chips. Once the processor chip in a computing node fail, memory data in this node can still be accessed by adjacent good nodes through memory network. It ensures the data

integrity and accuracy and improves the fault tolerance. The disadvantage of using independent memory chip is that the latency of memory access is increased mainly due to extra link latency of memory network.

So, how to reduce the link delay while keeping the bandwidth balance is very important. In order to optimize the bandwidth and latency of memory control chip, we do the research based on the traditional DDR3-1600 controller, and the conclusions are as follows: if only DDR3 memory devices are adopted, when two DDR3 controllers are integrated into memory control chip to realize two memory channels, the maximum performance efficient of each memory channel can be reached, and access latency can be controlled in an accepted range. Specific experiments and results analyzing will be presented in the third section of this paper.

### 2.2 The Design and Configuration of Memory Node

The important parts of memory node are memory control chip and memory network. The memory control chip in memory node is the same as the memory control chip in computing node. Each chip contains two DDR/NVM memory controllers. The router is the kernel of the memory network, and its basic function is to build the data path among memory controller modules in memory node, so as to realize the global data communication. The address mapping module is integrated into memory node to support the read and write operations to local or remote memory. The router is realized as 5 * 5 crossbar. A 2D mesh network with a topology of 2 rows and 4 columns can be constructed. The memory node has certain fault-tolerance ability: First, 2D mesh memory network can tolerate fault because routing algorithm has fault-tolerant ability. Even if several links between routers are down, data can still be transferred from other paths from source to destination. Second, there are two independent DDR/NVM memory controllers in one memory control chip and one can work as the backup of the other to improve the reliability.

These two memory controllers can be configured in four operating modes, as shown in Fig. 4. The memory control chip is abbreviated to MemCtrl Chip.

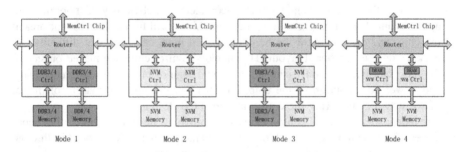

**Fig. 4.** Different configuration modes of memory node

**Mode one.** Two memory controllers are all configured to use DDR memory controller and use DRAM memory device. This mode is based on mature technology and the realization is simple. It has virtue that good compatibility with existing system architecture, and has disadvantages of higher power consumption of DRAM device and the volatile characteristic. The DRAM need to be refreshed periodically and all data in memory need to be written back to the hard disk (HDD) at last to prevent the data loss which will affect the efficiency of memory system.

**Mode two.** Two memory controllers are all configured to use NVM memory controller and use NVM memory device. The advantages of this mode are that the NVM has characters of non-volatile and low power consumption, so the memory consumption is reduced significantly and the overhead of backup can be avoided. The disadvantage of this mode is that the performance and durability of NVM are less than DRAM, in addition, the latency, power consumption and life time of read and write operations are not balance.

**Mode three.** DRAM and NVM are used together. Two channels use DDR and NVM channels respectively. During the execution of application, according to the profile of memory access, the data that are read and written frequently will be stored in DRAM, and the data that are seldom accessed will be stored in NVM. This mode not only can reach the high speed of DRAM, but also can take full advantage of characteristics of low power consumption and non-volatile of NVM.

**Mode four.** Both NVM and DRAM are used, NVM is used as main memory, and DRAM is used as the cache or buffer of NVM, which combines the characteristics of large capacity of NVM and high speed of DRAM. The NVM memory with large capacity can meet the growing demand for memory capacity, and faster DRAM memory as read and write cache or buffer can compensate for the lack of speed of NVM. It is more complex for this mode to be realized that special design for data allocation, replacement strategy and write merge mechanism should be considered.

In our opinion, the third mode has certain advantages from the perspective of not only hardware implementation but also software usage. Compared with the first mode, it can reduce power consumption and improve the reliability under the premise of ensuring performance. Compared with the second mode, it can avoid the problem of access latency being increased significantly when only NVM memory device is used. Compared with the forth mode, due to DRAM and NVM using independent channels respectively, so the control is easier and complexity is lower. However, there are still some problems to be solved when the third mode is implemented, including data distribution, data transfer, wear leveling, reliability control, and so on. For data distribution, a mechanism should be provided which can judge the data access frequency, and place the data accessed frequently into DRAM, place the data read more often but written fewer into NVM. For data transfer, by counting the numbers of read and write operations to different type of memory devices, the data can be transferred between DRAM and NVM according some optimization strategy. For wear leveling and reliability control, taking into account the read life and write lift of NVM, the number of write operation to NVM should be reduced as much as possible to increase the life time of NVM and avoid the performance loss due to longer write latency.

## 2.3    Latency and Bandwidth Optimization for CHMA

Compared with the traditional memory architecture, though CHMA can allocate larger memory capacity for the application, it has some problems yet. The most significant two problems are as following: one is increased memory latency and latency imbalance to different location of memory device; the other is bandwidth matching design between the processor chip and memory chip. In order to optimize the latency and bandwidth of interconnection path between chips, we propose the following two optimization techniques.

**Multi-channel parallel bus.** According to the analysis of the memory access behavior for typical applications, we find that the number of read commands is more than the number of write commands normally, and the write command can be optimized by delayed write and write merge. Therefore, the read response data bandwidth become the bottleneck. So, we put forward the multi-channel parallel bus that is different with traditional DDR3 bus. As shown in Fig. 5, two independent bus are located between the processor chip and the memory control chip, one is command (CMD) bus and the other is data (DATA) bus. The command bus charge to send the read and write command from the processor chip to memory chip, the data bus is responsible for returning the read response data from the memory control chip to the processor chip. The command bus and data bus are single direction which need not time-sharing, and only read response data are transferred through data bus. Through the further analysis of memory access characteristics for typical application such as stream, we find that the ratio of write and read commands is about 1:2. So, in order to reduce the bus width, save the chip pins and facilitate physical design, we suggest the width of CMD bus is half the width of the DATA bus, not only the application demand for bandwidth can be satisfied, but also the bandwidth of the CMD and DATA bus can be balanced. For DDR3 memory device, the latency of switching between read and write operation is larger, so continuous read commands or continuous write commands should be sent to the memory control chip as many as possible in order to improve the utilization rate of the data bus at most. The memory interface is responsible for scheduling commands according to this principle.

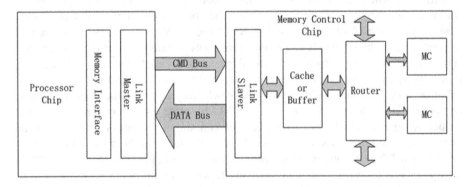

**Fig. 5.** Schematic diagram of multi-channel parallel bus

**Adding the Cache or Buffer structure in memory control chip.** Cache or Buffer structure is added in memory control chip to cache the data read out from memory and optimize the write command in order to reduce the memory access latency and improve the utilization of the CMD and DATA buses, as shown in Fig. 5. The data are saved at the granularity of a cacheline or a page. Storing data with page granularity can fully facilitate the characteristics of DDR3 memory device. It is more suitable to the applications which have a large number of contiguous data accessed to memory, such as stream program, to get a good optimization effect.

A virtual open page buffer (VOPB) is proposed in this paper to solve the problem of that the active pages in DRAM devices are switched frequently when multiple threads access the memory simultaneously. VOPB can reduce the number of memory accesses and page switching. Figure 6 is a schematic diagram of VOPB which is added between the memory access interface and memory control chip. VOPBs are placed in the memory control chip, and each memory control chip has an independent VOPB. Each VOPB is divided into 8 individual banks which saves the active pages from the corresponding banks of the DDR3 DIMM. Every active page stored in VOPB is called a virtual open page (VOP), which is consistent with the active page in the physical DIMM, as a physical copy of active page. Each bank of VOPB can hold 16 virtual active pages, each page size is 128 Byte, and the total capacity of VOPB is 16 KByte. VOPB receives memory access requests from the processor cores and determine the type of requests to memory controller. The size of request data from the cores is cacheline, and VOPB can change the request data size from cacheline to page by a prediction mechanism. A complete physical page will read from DDR3 DIMM, and store in VOPB as a virtual active page.

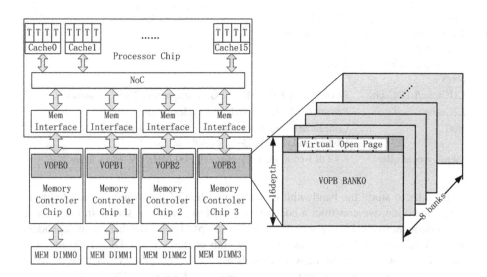

**Fig. 6.** Schematic diagram of VOPB

The VOPB has two obvious functions:

- reducing the number of access to DRAM by caching the active open pages if VOPB hits;
- page switching overhead of DRAM will be saved especially in the case of multiple address streams access the DRAM at the same time, by predicting cacheline access to stream access and caching multiple active pages to improve the hit ratio of VOPB.

In conclusion, with the restriction of the number of physical active pages in external memory, VOPB can provides extra virtual open pages for each bank of DRAM memory, increasing the total number of active pages, making up for the limitation of memory controller scheduling strategy for multi-thread processor, avoiding the active page switching frequently during multiple threads access memory at the same time.

## 3    Experimental Environment and Result Analysis

We use a multi-core multithreading CPU simulation environment MGTE [25] which is a self-developed simulation experiments to experiment. MGTE can simulate 16 cores and 128 threads at most. The processor cores, on-chip network, on chip memory system can use real Verilog codes or be replaced with fast models, the DDR3 memory controller and the DIMM uses the function models provided by IP vendor. The key architecture parameters of CPU in MGTE simulator are shown in Table 1.

**Table 1.** Key architecture parameters of CPU in MGTE simulator

| Unit | Parameter |
| --- | --- |
| The number of cores/threads | Simulator: 16/128 |
| The frequency of cores | 2 GHz |
| L1ICache/L1DCache | Privative, 64 KB/64 KB, 2 GHz frequency, 2 cycles latency |
| L2Cache | Privative, 512 KB, 2 GHz, 12 cycles latency |
| NoC | Concentrated mesh network, $7 \times 7$ router, 4 physical channel, 256 bits/channel, 2 GHz, 3–12 cycles latency |
| Memory controller | 8 DDR3-1600 memory channel, 800 MHz, 79–88 ns latency |

In order to study the bandwidth matching problem of the memory control chip in computing node, we construct a computing node test system as shown in Fig. 7. The test system includes 16 cores and 4 memory chips. Each core has an independent private L2Cache models, and each memory chip contains two DDR3-1600 memory controllers. NoC or memory network models are used to data communication between chips. Two ways can be supported for communication between L2Caches and memory control chips, one is through the NoC and memory network, the other is completely dependent on the memory network. Memory controllers in memory control chip are set according to standard DDR3 controller configurations. Two ranks and eight banks are included in each DDR3 DIMM in simulation. Each L2Cache model supports 4 threads to send four memory access flows at the same time, and can send read and write requests with continuous cacheline addresses or random addresses. The ratio of read to write can be set. The requests from different threads can be distributed uniformly to different DDR3 bank. Because the distance from one L2Cache to different memory control chip is different, therefore, different latency is set according to the distance. For a DDR3 memory controller, the network latency from the nearest L2Cache is set to 6 clock cycles, from the nearer L2Cache is set to 16 clock cycles, and from the farthest L2Cache is set to 20 clock cycles.

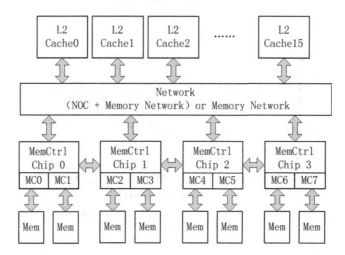

**Fig. 7.** Diagram of computing node test system

### 3.1  Experiment on Bandwidth Matching for Memory Access Interface

We analyze the average access time and access bandwidth through experiments. First, 16 L2Cache models are set to send memory access requests at the same time, Each L2Cache model is set to contain 4 threads, so a total of 64 threads send requests and produce 64 address streams to memory system. Second, 4 memory control chips which support 8 memory channels are set to receive the requests from 16 L2Caches. Each memory channel has 8 banks, so 64 banks are supported totally. Each thread is restricted to access a separate bank only. We define the L2C request density as the number of requests sent from L2Cache on average per 100 cycles. For example, request access density of 8 indicates 8 access requests on average will be sent per 100 clock cycles. The read and write requests of L2Cache can be sent at random in a certain proportion, and the ratio of read requests number to write requests number can be set from 1 to 4. The CMD link is set to 32-bits double-data-rate bus, and the DATA link is set to 64-bit double-data-rate bus. The frequency of them is 800 MHz. The test results are shown in Fig. 8.

128     H. Zhou et al.

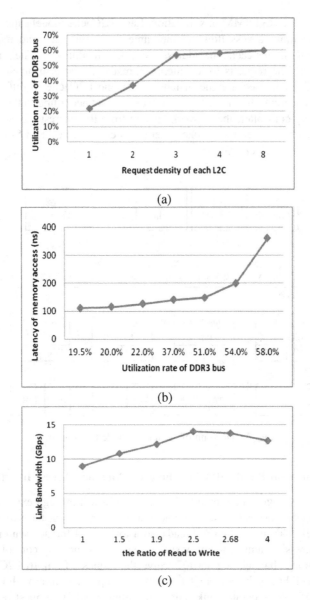

**Fig. 8.** Test experiment results of bandwidth and latency in memory interface

Figure 8(a) shows the change of DDR3 bus utilization rate when L2C request density is increased. As shown, with the request density increasing, the utilization rate of the DDR3 bus increases gradually. When the request density reaches, and exceeds 5, the utilization rate of the DDR3 bus is saturated, no more than 60%. Figure 8(b) illustrates the relationship between DDR3 bus utilization rate and memory latency. With the increasing of DDR bus utilization rate, memory latency increases gradually.

When the DDR bus utilization rate reaches saturation value, if L2C requests density is further increased, the memory latency is increased dramatically. The curve of memory latency changes with DDR bus utilization rate will reach the inflection point where the DDR bus utilization rate is 51%. According to the experiment, the following conclusion can be drawn: if the 64 threads and 8 DDR channels contained in processor node, in order to reduce memory latency, each DDR3-1600 channel bus utilization rate should not exceed 50%.

According to this conclusion, for the memory control chip, it is better to select two DDR3 channels as a group contained in one memory control chip, with a peak bandwidth of 25.6 GBps (128 bits * 800 MHz * 2 = 25.6 GBps). According to the experimental results, the effective bandwidth of each DDR3-1600 memory channel is about 50% of peak bandwidth, so the effective bandwidth of two DDR3-1600 channels together is 12.8 GBps (25.6 GBps * 50% = 12.8 GBps) approximately.

In our experiment, the access link between the processor chip and the memory control chip includes CMD and DATA links. The peak bandwidth of the CMD link is 6.4 GBps (32 bits * 800 MHz * 2 = 6.4 GBps), and the peak bandwidth of the DATA link is 12.8 GBps (64 bits * 800 MHz * 2 = 12.8 GBps), so the total peak bandwidth is 19.2 GBps. The relationship between link effective bandwidth and the ratio of memory read to write is shown in Fig. 8(c). When the ratio of read to write is 2.5, the effective bandwidth of the link can reach 14 GBps, and it is equivalent with the effective bandwidth of 12.8 GBps that two DDR3-1600 channel can provide. It means that the CMD and DATA links can satisfy the requirements of latency and bandwidth between processor chip and memory control chip and do not become the bottleneck of bandwidth.

## 3.2 Performance of VOPB in Memory Control Chip

In order to evaluate the actual performance optimization effect on VOPB when it is added in memory control chip, 64-thread Stream OpenMP [26] and NPB-MPI test benches [27] are used to test in MGTE simulation environment. For the 64-thread Stream OpenMP program, each thread is set to access all memory channels uniformly. Because the number of access is fixed, so memory effective bandwidth is used to measure the effect of VOPB. Higher the memory bandwidth is, shorter the execution time will be. The test results of 64-thread stream copy, scale, add and triad programs are shown in Fig. 9(a). As shown, after VOPBs are used, the total effective memory bandwidth is improved from 12.29 GBps to 14.37 GBps on average, the ratio of increasing is about 16.86%. For NPB-MPI test benches set, the number of million operations per second (Mop/s per second) is used the index to measure the execution performance of program with VOPB. For comparing conveniently, the execution performance when no VOPB is used is defined as the base value. The normalized execution performance is defined as the real execution performance when VOPBs are used is divided by the base value. The test results for NPB-MPI are shown in Fig. 9(b). As shown, for the NPB-MPI test benches set, the performance is increased up to 6% on average when VOPBs are used.

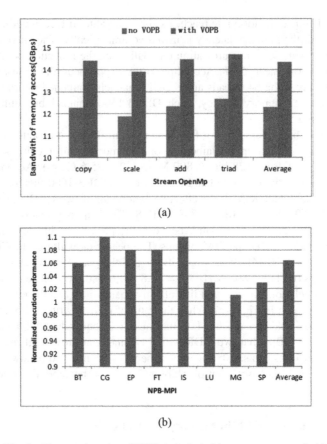

(a)

(b)

**Fig. 9.** Test results when VOPB is included in memory control chip

## 4   Conclusion

This paper presents a configurable hybrid memory architecture (CHMA) for large data processing, including the computing nodes and the memory nodes. The computing node provide computing resources for computing system of data processing, can be configured to appropriate mode according to the special needs of computing ability for different application to improve the applicability of the calculation system. The memory node contains memory control chip and memory network, each memory control chip contains two memory controllers, supporting different types of memory devices to build hybrid memory system. The network router integrated in memory control chip supports to set up memory network with various topologies. For the problem of delay and bandwidth optimization for CHMA, two key technologies of the multi-channel parallel bus and stream buffer in memory control chip are proposed and experiments are done to verify their optimization effects. The experimental results show that: first, the integration of the two DDR3-1600 memory controllers in one memory control chip can maximize the bandwidth utilization of each memory channel; second, the bandwidth of proposed multi-channel parallel bus can reach balance with effective bandwidth of two DDD3-1600 channels; third, adding a stream buffer in memory control chip can reduce the memory delay and improve memory bandwidth. The experimental results show that for 64-thread Stream OpenMP program the memory bandwidth is increased by 16.86%, for 64-thread NPB-MPI scientific computing applications the speed is improved up to 6% on average. The experimental results have theoretical significance and engineering realization value for designing memory computing system for large data processing.

# References

1. Koomey, J.: Estimating Total power consumption by servers in the U.S. and the World. Lawrence Berkeley National Laboratory, USA (2007)
2. 288 Mb SIO Reduced Latency (RLDRAM II) Datasheet [DB/OL] (2003). http://www. micron.com
3. Kalla, R., Sinharoy, B., Starke, W., Floyd, M.: POWER7: IBM's next-generation server processor. IEEE Micro 30(2), 7–15 (2010)
4. Zhao, W., Belhaire, E., Mistral, Q., et al.: Macro-model of spin-transfer torque based magnetic tunnel junction device for hybrid magnetic–CMOS design. In: IEEE International Behavioral Modeling and Simulation Workshop, pp. 40–43 (2006)
5. Sun, G., Dong, X., Xie, Y., Li, J., Chen, Y.: A novel architecture of the 3D stacked MRAM L2 cache for CMPs. In: High Performance Computer Architecture, pp. 239–249, February 2009
6. Hanzawa, S., Kitai, N., Osada, K., Kotabe, A., et al.: A 512 KB embedded phase change memory with 416 kB/s write throughput at 100 uA cell write current. In: IEEE International Solid-State Circuits Conference, pp. 474–616 (2007)
7. Chung, L.: Cell design considerations for phase change memory as a universal memory. In: International Symposium on VLSI Technology, Systems and Applications, pp. 132–133 (2008)
8. Chen, Y.S., Lee, H.Y., et al.: Highly scalable hafnium oxide memory with improvements of resistive distribution and read disturb immunity. In: Proceeding of the International Electron Devices Meeting, pp. 105–108 (2009)
9. Sheu, S.S., Chang, M.F., Lin, K.F., et al.: A 4 Mb embedded SLC resistive-RAM macro with 7.2 ns read-write random-access time and 160 ns MLC-access capability. In: Proceeding of the IEEE International Solid-State Circuit Conference, pp. 200–201 (2011)
10. Zhou, P., Zhao, B., Yang, J., Zhang, Y.: A durable and energy efficient main memory using phase change memory technology. In: International Symposium on Computer Architecture (ISCA 2009), pp. 14–32, June 2009
11. Lee, B.C., Zhou, P., Yang, J., Zhang, Y., Zhao, B., Ipek, E., Mutlu, O., Burger, D.: Phase-change technology and the future of main memory. IEEE Micro 30(1), 143 (2010)
12. Wu, X., Li, J., Zhang, L., et al.: Design exploration of hybrid caches with disparate memory technologies. ACM Trans. Archit. Code Optim. 7(3) (2010)
13. Wu, X., Li, J., Zhang, L., et al.: Power and performance of read-write aware hybrid caches with non-volatile memories. In: Proceeding of the Conference on Design, Automation and Test in Europe, pp. 737–742 (2009)
14. Valero, A., Sahuquillo, J., petit, S., et al.: A hybrid eDRAM/SDRAM macrocell. In: Annual IEEE/ACM International Symposium on Microarchitecture, pp. 213–221 (2009)

15. Yu, W.S., Huang, R., Xu, S.Q., et al.: SRAM-DRAM hybrid memory with application to efficient register files in fine-grained multi-threading. In: International Symposium on Computer Architecture (ISCA 2011), pp. 247–258, June 2011

16. Caulfield, A.M., De, A., Coburn, J., et al.: Moneta: a high-performance storage array architecture for next-generation, non-volatile memories. In: Proceedings of the International Symposium on Microarchitecture, pp. 385–395 (2010)

17. Zhou, P., Zhao, B., Yang, J., Zhang, Y.: Energy reduction for STT-RAM using early write termination. In: Proceedings of the International Conference on Computer-Aided Design, pp. 264–268 (2009)

18. Qureshi, M.K., Franceschini, M., Lastras, L.: Improving read performance of phase change memories via write cancellation and write pausing. In: Proceedings of the International Symposium on High Performance Computer Architecture, pp. 1–11 (2010)

19. Mogul, J.C., Argollo, E., Shah, M., Faraboschi, P.: Operating system support for NVM +DRAM hybrid main memory. In: The 12th Workshop on Hot Topics in Operating Systems (HatOS XII), pp. 18–20, May 2009

20. Make full use of the powerful SAP HANA memory computing platform [DB/OL] (2015). http://www.sap.com/china/pc/tech/in-memory-computing-hana.html

21. Engineered System for Extreme Analytics [DB/OL] (2015). https://www.oracle.com/engineered-systems/exalytics/index.html

22. Ousterhout, J.: RAMCloud: Scalable High-Performance Storage Entirely in DRAM [DB/OL]. Stanford University (2009). http://www.cs.uci.edu/bin/pdf/seminarseries2011/RAMCloud-Irvine.pdf

23. Huang, L., Wang, Z., Xiao, N., Wang, Y., Dou, Q.: Integrated coherence prediction: towards efficient cache coherence on NoC-based multicore architectures. ACM Trans. Des. Autom. Electron. Syst. (TODAES) 19(3) (2014)

24. Li, C., Ma, S., Chen, S., et al.: Express ring: a multi-layer and non-blocking NoC architecture. IEICE Electron. Express 12(3), 1–12 (2015)

25. Yan, X., Deng, R., Sun, C., Dou, Q.: MGTE: a multi-level hybrid verification platform for a 16-core processor. In: Xu, W., Xiao, L., Lu, P., Li, J., Zhang, C. (eds.) NCCET 2012. CCIS, vol. 337, pp. 16–26. Springer, Heidelberg (2013). https://doi.org/10.1007/978-3-642-35898-2_3

26. Mallón, D.A., et al.: Performance evaluation of MPI, UPC and OpenMP on multicore architectures. In: Ropo, M., Westerholm, J., Dongarra, J. (eds.) EuroPVM/MPI 2009. LNCS, vol. 5759, pp. 174–184. Springer, Heidelberg (2009). https://doi.org/10.1007/978-3-642-03770-2_24

27. Van der Wijngaart, R.F., Wong, P.: NAS parallel benchmarks version 2.4 [DB/OL]. NAS Technical report: NAS-02-2007 (2002)

# An Efficient Model for Soft Error Vulnerability of Dynamic Circuits

Yan Sun$^{(\boxtimes)}$, Yuesheng Cao, Jinwen Li, and Tiejun Li

College of Computer, National University of Defense Technology,
Changsha 410073, Hunan, People's Republic of China
yansun@nudt.edu.cn

**Abstract.** Dynamic circuits are widely used in high-speed circuit. However, dynamic circuits are very vulnerable to soft errors. An analytical model of critical charge for vulnerable nodes of dynamic circuits is developed. As the accurate model is too complex to calculate, a simplified efficient model is proposed by using an approximate method. Proposed model are verified by SPICE simulation and error analysis respectively. Results demonstrate that these models have high accuracy and can be used both in the efficient analysis and automatic CAD tools.

**Keywords:** Soft error · Dynamic circuit · Critical charge
Domino logic

## 1 Introduction

Dynamic circuits are widely used in high performance design because of their increased speed and reduced implementation area, such as ALUs, register files, and multiplexers. However, with the progress of VLSI technology, the scaling down of supply voltage and feature size increase the vulnerability of circuits to soft errors, and especially worsen the reliability of dynamic circuits [1].

The objective of this paper is to character and quantify the impact of soft errors on dynamic circuits. The profile of soft error vulnerability in dynamic circuits is studied, then an accurate and an efficient model for soft error vulnerability estimation of dynamic circuits are proposed.

## 2 Vulnerability Profile of Dynamic Circuits

Domino logic is widespread representative of dynamic logic, we will refer to domino logic as the typical dynamic circuits in this paper. A domino logic module

This work was supported by the National High-Tech Research and Development Program of China (No. 2015AA01A301), the National Natural Science Foundation of China (No. 61303069), and the Ministry of Education Doctoral Foundation of China (No. 20124307110016).

W. Xu et al. (Eds.): NCCET 2017, CCIS 600, pp. 133–142, 2018.
https://doi.org/10.1007/978-981-10-7844-6_13

consists of an n-type dynamic logic block followed by a static inverter, and it has two phases of operation. In the precharge phase, the output of the dynamic gate is charged to logic "1"; in the evaluate phase, the output node either remains at "1" or discharged to "0" depending on inputs. Figure 1 shows a domino inverter chain. Cha *et al.* reported that any gate can be always mapped into equivalent inverters [2], so in this paper a domino inverter chain is taken as an example to research the character of dynamic circuits' vulnerability to soft errors.

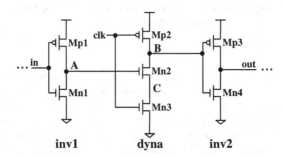

**Fig. 1.** A segment of a domino inverter chain.

In combinational circuits, single event transient (SET) becomes a dominant source of soft errors [3]. A SET may propagate to a flip-flop input and get latched. Same as critical charge defined for memory elements, the SET critical charge ($Q_{SET}$) can be defined as the minimum amount of collected charges at a circuit node which may give rise to a SET in subsequent gate [4]. A typical domino inverter chain is made up of a group of dynamic and static CMOS inverters, as shown in Fig. 1. In order to estimate vulnerability of it, just need to analyze characters of nodes A, B and C.

When an SET occurs at node A, B or C, the impact on output is various. It can be classified into 12 cases, as shown in Table 1. $Q_{SET}$ of case B1, B3, C1 are almost the same and $Q_{SET,B3} < Q_{SET,B1} < Q_{SET,C1}$; $Q_{SET}$ of case C2, C3, C4 are rather larger. Therefore, in order to estimate soft error vulnerability of domino inverter chain, only need to analyze $Q_{SET}$ of A4, B2, B3 and B4.

## 3   Vulnerability Quantitative Modeling of Dynamic Circuits

A particle strikes in susceptible nodes can cause a transient current impulse. To analyze soft error vulnerability, the transient current impulse can be described as a rectangular pulse with amplitude $I_0$ and width $t_m$.

### 3.1   Case A4, B2 and B3

Set static and dynamic inverters of circuit in Fig. 1 to be minimal size. For case A4, a particle strike in node A can cause a positive current impulse when $in = 1$ and $clk = 1$, and the impulse can be described by Eq. (1).

**Table 1.** Soft error vulnerabilities of susceptible nodes in a domino inverter chain

| Case | $in$ | $clk$ | Polarity of SET | Impact on out | $Q_{SET}$ |
|------|------|-------|-----------------|---------------|-----------|
| A1 | 0 | 0 | Negative | No impact | Infinite |
| A2 | 0 | 1 | Negative | No impact | Infinite |
| A3 | 1 | 0 | Positive | No impact | Infinite |
| A4 | 1 | 1 | Positive | $0 \to 1$ | Small |
| B1 | 0 | 0 | Negative | $0 \to 1 \to 0$ | Small |
| B2 | 0 | 1 | Positive | $1 \to 0 \to 1$ | Small |
| B3 | 1 | 0 | Negative | $0 \to 1 \to 0$ | Small |
| B4 | 1 | 1 | Negative | $0 \to 1$ | Very small |
| C1 | 0 | 0 | Negative | $0 \to 1 \to 0$ | Small |
| C2 | 0 | 1 | Positive | $1 \to 0 \to 1$ | Large |
| C3 | 1 | 0 | Negative | $0 \to 1 \to 0$ | Large |
| C4 | 1 | 1 | Negative | $0 \to 1$ | Large |

$$I_a(t) = G_{n1}V_a(t) + C_{tot,a}\frac{dV_a(t)}{dt}, \tag{1}$$

where $G_{n1}$ is conductance of Mn1. $C_{tot,a}$ is total capacitance of node A. For case A4, $C_{tot,a}$ is sum of diffusion capacitance of Mp1 and Mn1, and gate capacitance of Mn2. When $0 \le t \le t_m$, voltage of node A can be solved:

$$V_a(t) = \frac{I_0}{G_{n1}}\left[1 - \exp\left(-\frac{G_{n1}}{C_{tot,a}}t\right)\right]. \tag{2}$$

Once voltage of node A overtakes switch threshold of devices followed, SET generated in node A would propagate to next stage. In this case, the minimal collected charge is $Q_{SET}$ of node A. If switch threshold of devices followed node A is $V_T$, the critical condition of SET propagate to next stage is $V_a(t_m) = V_T$. In Fig. 1, $V_T$ is threshold voltage of transistor Mn2, $V_{T,n2}$. Accumulated charge reaches to maximum at time $t_m$. Take $t = t_m$ to Eq. (2) and $I_{0,t_m}$ can be solved:

$$I_{0,t_m} = \frac{V_{T,n2}G_{n1}}{1 - \exp\left(\frac{-t_mG_{n1}}{C_{tot,a}}\right)}. \tag{3}$$

And then, the $Q_{SET}$ of case A4 can be calculated:

$$Q_{SET,A4} = \frac{V_{T,n2}t_mG_{n1}}{1 - \exp\left(\frac{-t_mG_{n1}}{C_{tot,a}}\right)}. \tag{4}$$

Using the same method, $Q_{SET,B2}$ and $Q_{SET,B3}$ also can be solved:

$$Q_{SET,B2} = \frac{V_{T,inv2}t_mG_{n2,n3}}{1 - \exp\left(\frac{-t_mG_{n2,n3}}{C_{tot,b}}\right)}, \tag{5}$$

$$Q_{\text{SET,B3}} = \frac{(V_{DD} - V_{T,inv2})t_m G_{p2}}{1 - \exp\left(\dfrac{-t_m G_{p2}}{C_{tot,b}}\right)}. \tag{6}$$

In Eqs. (5) and (6), $V_{T,inv2}$ is switch threshold of inv2; $G_{n2,n3}$ is conductance of Mn2-Mn3 pull-down path; $C_{tot,b}$ is total capacitance of node B; $V_{DD}$ is supply voltage; $G_{p2}$ is conductance of Mp2. It can be found that $Q_{\text{SET}}$ of case A4, B2 and B3 have similar expression, and they can be united to one equation:

$$Q_{\text{SET}} = \frac{V_T^* t_m G_d}{1 - \exp\left(\dfrac{-t_m G_d}{C_{tot}}\right)}, \tag{7}$$

where $G_d$ is drive transistors conductance of target node; $C_{tot}$ is total capacitance of target node; $V_T^*$ is switch threshold of next stage, which is $V_{DD} - V_T$ or $V_T$ for particular cases. Generally, drive transistors work in linear area, therefore $G_d$ in Eq. (7) can be expressed approximately as:

$$G_d = \mu C_{ox} \frac{W}{L}(V_{GS} - V_T) = k_g W, \tag{8}$$

where $\mu$ is mobility of electron or hole; $C_{ox}$ is capacitance of gate oxide per unit area; $V_T$ is threshold voltage of transistors; $W$ and $L$ is equivalent channel width and length of transistors respectively. $k_g$ is a constant related to technology and circuit, which can be expressed as $k_g = \mu C_{ox}(V_{GS} - V_T)/L$.

Assume that number of transistors source or drain connected to target node is $n$, and gate connected to target node is $r$. Equation (7) can be written as:

$$C_{tot} = \sum_{i=1}^{n} C_{diff,i} + \sum_{j=1}^{r} C_{G,j}, \tag{9}$$

where $\sum_{i=1}^{n} C_{diff,i}$ is total diffusion capacitance of target node; $\sum_{j=1}^{r} C_{G,j}$ is total gate capacitance of target node. For a single MOSFET, $C_{diff} = C_j LW + C_{jsw}(2L + W) = k_{c0} + k_{c1}W$, and $C_G = (C_{ox}L + 2C_o)W = k_{c2}W$. Where $C_j$, $C_{jsw}$, $C_{ox}$ and $C_o$ are technology constant. In addition, channel length of transistors are minimum value. Consequently, $k_{c0}$, $k_{c1}$ and $k_{c2}$ are constant.

According to Eq. (7), $Q_{\text{SET}}$ of case A4, B2 and B3 can be expressed as:

$$Q_{\text{SET}} = \frac{V_T^* t_m k_g W_d}{1 - \exp\left(\dfrac{-t_m k_g W_d}{\sum_{i=1}^{n}(k_{c0,i} + k_{c1,i}W_i) + \sum_{j=1}^{r}(k_{c2,j}W_j)}\right)}, \tag{10}$$

where $W_d$ is equivalent channel width of transistors in drive logic; $W_i$ is channel width of transistors connected to target node in drive logic; $W_j$ is channel width of transistors in fan-out logic. Other variables are all constant and are related to technology and circuit structure.

## 3.2    Case B4

For case B4, both Mp2 and Mn2 are closed. A negative impulse would be generated when a particle strikes in node B. Because node B doesn't have path to supply or ground, the current can be described in Eq. (11):

$$C_{tot} = \sum_{i=1}^{n} C_{diff,i} + \sum_{j=1}^{r} C_{G,j}, \tag{11}$$

where $C_{tot,b}$ is total capacitance of node B. When $0 \leq t \leq t_m$, $I_b(t) = I_0$. Voltage of node B can be expressed:

$$V_b(t) = \frac{1}{C_{tot,b}} \int_0^t I_b(t)dt = \frac{I_0}{C_{tot,b}}t. \tag{12}$$

Once the voltage of node B overtakes switch threshold of devices followed, SET generated in node B would propagate to next stage. In this case, the minimal collected charge is $Q_{SET}$ of node B. If switch threshold of devices followed node B is $V_{DD} - V_{T,nv2}$, the critical condition of SET propagate to next stage is $V_b(t_m) = V_{DD} - V_{T,inv2}$. Accumulated charge of node B reaches to maximum at time $t_m$, so the $Q_{SET}$ of case B4 can be calculated:

$$Q_{SET,B4} = \frac{C_{tot,b}(V_{DD} - V_{T,inv2})}{t_m}t_m = C_{tot,b}(V_{DD} - V_{T,inv2}). \tag{13}$$

Because source or drain of Mp2 and Mn2 are connected to node B, gate of Mp3 and Mn4 are connected to node B, Eq. (14) can be solved:

$$C_{tot,b} = (C_{diff,p2} + C_{diff,n2}) + (C_{G,p3} + C_{G,n4}). \tag{14}$$

Same as case A4, $Q_{SET}$ of case B4 can be expressed:

$$Q_{SET} = \Big[ (k_{c0,p2} + k_{c1,p2}W_{p2}) + (k_{c0,n2} + k_{c1,n2}W_{n2})$$
$$+ (k_{c2,p3}W_{p3} + k_{c2,n4}W_{n4}) \Big] (V_{DD} - V_{T,inv2}), \tag{15}$$

where $W_{p2}$, $W_{n2}$, $W_{p3}$ and $W_{n4}$ are effective channel width of Mp2, Mn2, Mp3 and Mn4, respectively. Other variables are constant related to technology and circuit structure.

From above analysis, $Q_{SET}$ of vulnerable nodes in dynamic circuits are only related to transistor size for a certain technology and circuit structure. Transistor sizing is an effective technique to improve $Q_{SET}$ of vulnerable nodes [5], thereby reduce vulnerability to soft errors of dynamic circuits.

## 4    Model Simplifying for Vulnerability of Dynamic Circuits

SET critical charges of vulnerable nodes can be calculated using Eqs. (10) and (15) accurately. However, accurate model is too complex to calculate, especially for case A4, B2 and B3. It is necessary to research simpler model for efficient analyzing and automatic CAD tools.

For a certain technology and circuit structure, $Q_{\text{SET}}$ is only related to channel width of drive and load transistors when channel length of transistors are minimum value, and PMOS-NMOS in inv1, dyna, inv2 are asymmetric structure. Set channel width of load (or drive) transistors as minimum size, and observe trends of $Q_{\text{SET}}$ with variation of channel width of drive (or load) transistors. It is can be found that the trends are approximately linear. Based on this observation, Eq. (10) can be simplified to:

$$Q_{\text{SET}}(W_d, W_f) \approx \cfrac{AW_d}{1 - \exp\left(\cfrac{-BW_d}{CW_d + DW_f + E}\right)}, \tag{16}$$

where $A$, $B$, $C$, $D$ and $E$ are parameters related to technology and circuit structure, and they are all positive numbers; $W_d$ and $W_f$ are equivalent channel width of drive transistors and load transistors, respectively. Because $B$ is much larger than $C$, $D$ and $E$, Eq. (16) can be expressed approximately as Eq. (17) when $W_f$ takes the minimum value $W_{f,min}$:

$$Q_{\text{SET}}(W_d, W_{f,\min}) \approx AW_d = V_T^* t_m k_g W_d. \tag{17}$$

For case A4, B2 and B3, $Q_{\text{SET}}$ of vulnerable nodes is proportional to $W_d$ approximately. $W_f$ can be ignored because $Q_{\text{SET}}$ is almost independent on it.

When $W_d$ is very small, make:

$$\frac{-BW_d}{CW_d + DW_f + E} = S, \tag{18}$$

Equation (16) can be transferred to:

$$Q_{\text{SET}}(W_d, W_f) \approx \cfrac{-A\cfrac{S(DW_f + E)}{SC + B}}{1 - \exp(S)}. \tag{19}$$

When $W_d$ is much smaller than $W_f$, it can be considered that $W_d \to 0$, so $S \to 0$. According to Maclaurin expansion, Eq. (19) can be expressed as:

$$Q_{\text{SET}}(W_d, W_f) \approx \frac{AS(DW_f + E)}{S^2 C + SB} \sim \frac{A}{B}(DW_f + E), \tag{20}$$

where $A/B = V_T^*$. Constant $E$ can be ignored as it is about 8~9 orders of magnitude smaller than $D$. When $W_d$ takes the minimum value $W_{d,min}$, Eq. (16) can be expressed as:

$$Q_{\text{SET}}(W_{d,\min}, W_f) \approx AW_{d,\min} + V_T^* DW_f, \tag{21}$$

where $A = V_T^* t_m k_g$, and $D = k_{c2}$, take them to Eq. (21):

$$Q_{\text{SET}}(W_{d,\min}, W_f) \approx V_T^* t_m k_g W_{d,\min} + V_T^* k_{c2} W_f, \tag{22}$$

where $k_{c2}$ is a constant related to gate capacitance of load transistor; the product of $t_m$ and $k_g$ is about one order of magnitude larger than $k_{c2}$. From this, we obtain the approximate expressions of $Q_{\text{SET}}(W_d, W_{f,min})$ and $Q_{\text{SET}}(W_{d,min}, W_f)$.

If $Q_{\text{SET}}(W_d, W_f)$ is a linear function with two unknown variables, it can be assumed:

$$Q_{\text{SET}}(W_d, W_f) = aW_d + bW_f + c, \tag{23}$$

where $a$, $b$ and $c$ are constant. If the expressions of $Q_{\text{SET}}(W_d, W_{f,min})$ and $Q_{\text{SET}}(W_{d,min}, W_f)$ are known, then:

$$\begin{aligned}
Q_{\text{SET}}(W_d, W_f) = &\, Q_{\text{SET}}(W_d, W_{f,\min}) + Q_{\text{SET}}(W_{d,\min}, W_f) \\
&- Q_{\text{SET}}(W_{d,\min}, W_{f,\min}).
\end{aligned} \tag{24}$$

Therefore, as long as we can prove that $Q_{\text{SET}}(W_d, W_f)$ is a linear function, we can get the expression. According to Eq. (10), $Q_{\text{SET}}$ in case A4, B2 and B3 can be expressed as a function of $W_d$ and $W_f$. Take technology parameters to the equation and obtain three-dimensional surfaces as shown in Fig. 2.

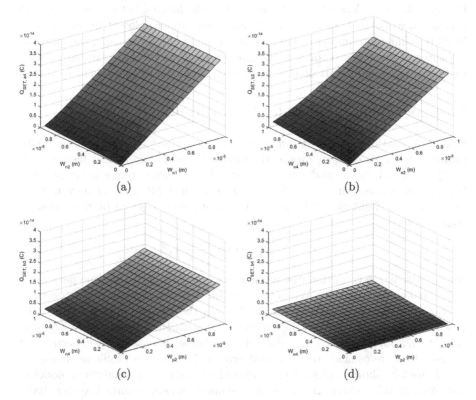

**Fig. 2.** Distribution of $Q_{\text{SET}}$ in case (a) A4, (b) B2, (c) B3 and (d) B4.

According to Fig. 2, surfaces (a), (b) and (c) are nearly flat. In the approximate calculation, $Q_{\text{SET}}$ can be roughly considered as a linear function of $W_d$ and $W_f$. Thus:

$$Q_{\text{SET}}(W_d, W_f) = V_T^* \left( t_m k_g W_d + k_{c2} W_f \right). \tag{25}$$

By now, an efficient model of $Q_{\text{SET}}$ in the case of A4, B2 and B3 is obtained.

For case B4, the model in Eq. (15) is already linear. Assume the ratio of $W_{p2}$ and $W_{n2}$ is $\alpha$, $W_{p3}$ and $W_{n4}$ is $\beta$. $Q_{\text{SET}}$ for case B4 can be expressed as:

$$Q_{\text{SET}} = \Big[ (k_{c0,p2} + k_{c0,n2}) + (\alpha k_{c1,p2} + k_{c1,n2}) W_{n2}$$
$$+ (\beta k_{c2,p3} + k_{c2,n4}) W_{n4} \Big] (V_{DD} - V_{T,inv2}). \tag{26}$$

In general, $k_{c0}$ can be ignored as its magnitude far less than $k_{c1}$ and $k_{c2}$. Let $\alpha k_{c1,p2} + k_{c1,n2} = k_{c1}$, $\beta k_{c2,p3} + k_{c2,n4} = k_{c2}$, $V_{DD} - V_{T,inv2} = V_T^*$, then:

$$Q_{\text{SET}}(W_d, W_f) = V_T^* \left( k_{c1} W_d + k_{c2} W_f \right). \tag{27}$$

Thus, a simplified model of $Q_{\text{SET}}$ for four cases is obtained. It is found that Eqs. (25) and (27) are identical except the coefficient $W_d$. In the case of A4, B2 and B3, $Q_{\text{SET}}$ depends mainly on the switch threshold of fan-out logic, the conductance of drive transistor and the gate capacitance of load transistor. $Q_{\text{SET}}$ in B4 is mainly determined by the switch threshold of fan-out logic, the diffusion capacitor of drive transistor and the gate capacitance of load transistor. In all cases, the $Q_{\text{SET}}$ is proportional to the switch threshold of subsequent logic.

## 5    Experiment and Model Verification

SPICE simulations and error analysis were performed to verify vulnerability profile of dynamic circuits, proposed analytical model and efficient model.

$Q_{\text{SET}}$ of vulnerable nodes were evaluated by current source injection. The benchmark experiment was performed in a 28 nm CMOS technology using a SPICE circuit simulation. The injected current source is given by the following equation [6]:

$$I(t) = \frac{Q}{T} \sqrt{\frac{t}{T}} \exp\left(-\frac{t}{T}\right), \tag{28}$$

where $Q$ is charge collection due to energetic particles; $T$ is the time parameter associated with technology. When the technology is determined, $T$ is a constant.

Figure 3(a) shows the $Q_{\text{SET}}$ distributions of the vulnerable nodes under various conditions in the current injection experiment. Results show that $Q_{\text{SET}}$ of A4, B1, B2, B3, B4, and C1 are relatively small in all cases, and the experimental distributions are coincide with the soft error vulnerabilities profile analysis.

Figure 3(b) shows a $Q_{\text{SET}}$ comparison of simulation and analytical model in case A4, B2, B3, and B4. x1 represents the minimum size domino inverter chain, and x4 and x8 represent the chain scaled by a factor of 4 and 8, respectively. The $Q_{\text{SET}}$ trend calculated by analytical model conforms to the SPICE simulation results, and errors are very small. Errors could be caused by three factors: $G_d$ and $C_{tot}$ are approximations; $t_m$ is slightly different from the actual situation; and $V_T^*$ varies with the actual operating point.

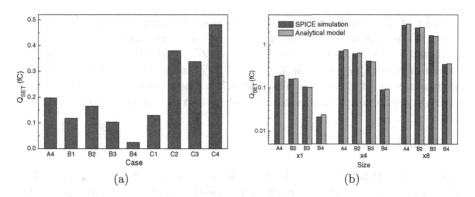

**Fig. 3.** (a) $Q_{SET}$ distributions, (b) SPICE simulation and analytical model.

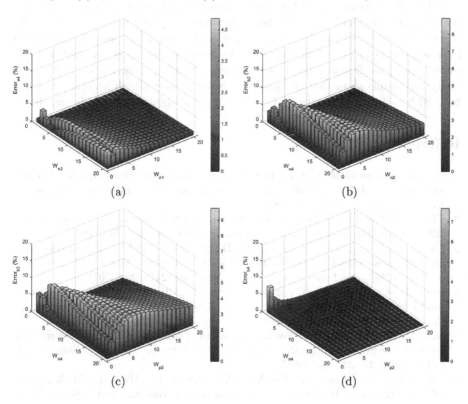

**Fig. 4.** Errors of efficient model in case (a) A4, (b) B2, (c) B3 and (d) B4.

To verify the accuracy of the simplified efficient model, results of the model were compared with the analytical model, and errors of the efficient model are analyzed. Figure 4 shows errors of $Q_{SET}$ calculated by analytical model and efficient model of case A4, B2, B3 and B4 in 28 nm CMOS technology.

142    Y. Sun et al.

In Fig. 4, the widths of drive and load transistors are in the range from 50 nm to 10 μm. We choose 20 × 20 groups error data for every case. In four cases, the maximum errors of $Q_{SET}$ are 4.86%, 8.82%, 9.65% and 7.68%, respectively. The average errors of $Q_{SET}$ are 1.48%, 3.72%, 5.13% and 0.19% respectively, and the maximum error of all cases is less than 9.7%. The model can meet the general accuracy requirements in approximate calculation of manual or CAD tools.

## 6  Conclusion

The soft error vulnerability of dynamic circuits is analyzed and studied, and an efficient analysis model of soft error vulnerability is proposed. Firstly, the profile of soft error vulnerability in dynamic circuit is analyzed. Then a quantitative model of SET critical charges for vulnerable nodes of dynamic circuits is deduced. As the precise model is too complex, a reasonable approximation of the model is made according to the specific situation, and a simplified and efficient model for the critical charge of sensitive nodes in dynamic circuits is deduced. Finally, experimental verification and error analysis are performed. Experimental and analytical results show that the proposed model achieves high accuracy and can be used for efficient estimation of soft error vulnerability of dynamic circuits.

## References

1. Kumar, J., Tahoori, M.B.: A low power soft error suppression technique for dynamic logic. In: 20th IEEE International Symposium on Defect and Fault Tolerance in VLSI Systems, pp. 454–462 (2005)
2. Cha, H., Patel, J.H.: A logic-level model for α-particle hits in CMOS circuits. In: IEEE International Conference on Computer Design, pp. 538–542 (1993)
3. Naseer, R., Draper, J., Boulghassoul, Y., Dasgupta, S., Witulski, A.: Critical charge and SET pulse widths for combinational logic in commercial 90 nm CMOS technology. In: ACM Great Lakes Symposium on VLSI, pp. 227–230 (2007)
4. Rossi, D., Cazeaux, J.M., Omana, M., Metra, C., Chatterjee, A.: Accurate linear model for SET critical charge estimation. IEEE Trans. Very Large Scale Integr. (VLSI) Syst. **17**, 1161–1166 (2009)
5. Raji, M., Ghavami, B.: Soft error rate reduction of combinational circuits using gate sizing in the presence of process variations. IEEE Trans. Very Large Scale Integr. (VLSI) Syst. **25**, 247–260 (2017)
6. Shivakumar, P., Kistler, M., Keckler, S.W., Burger, D., Alvisi, L.: Modeling the effect of technology trends on the soft error rate of combinational logic. In: International Conference on Dependable Systems and Networks, pp. 389–398 (2002)

# Author Index

Printed in the United States
By Bookmasters